THIS WAY UP

THE LOCAL OFFICIAL'S

HANDBOOK for PRIVATIZATION

and CONTRACTING OUT

Edited by
Raymond Q. Armington and William D. Ellis

Coordinated by
American Society of Local Officials, Inc.
721 Second Street, NE. Washington, DC
20002

REGNERY GATEWAY   CHICAGO

Published by Regnery Gateway, Inc
940–950 North Shore Drive
Lake Bluff, Illinois 60044

Library of Congress Cataloging in Publication Data
Main entry under title:

This way up.

    Bibliography: p.
    1. Municipal services—United States—Contracting out.
I. Armington, Raymond Q., 1907–   II. Ellis,
William Donohue. III. American Society of Local
Officials.
HD4605.T47   1984   352.1'61'0973   84-14371
ISBN 0-89526-824-8 (pbk.)

Dedicated to

those local government officials who make the whole
system function *pro bono publico*.

Acknowledging . . .

. . . the conscientious work of the authors of these chapters who each distilled the accumulated knowledge of a distinguished professional life into one valuable chapter. The work of Clyde Peters of Regnery Gateway, Inc., in bringing this project together. The work of Leila Adamoski, Regnery Gateway, in production of this book. The work of Pauline Griffitts Fanslow, of Editorial, Inc., in editorial handling of this complex manuscript.

William D. Ellis
and
Raymond Q. Armington

Subsidiarity

"Let no public organization take
over a problem which can be
handled by a private one. Let
no higher echelon of government
take over what a lower can perform."

—a revered principle of
ancient Greek government.

CONTENTS

PREFACE

This book is the action-oriented companion volume to the book, *MORE: The Rediscovery of American Common Sense.*

MORE, using examples you will recognize, demonstrates the power of unleashing the creative initiative of individuals and the private sector.

THIS WAY UP: The Local Official's Handbook for Privatization and Contracting Out goes on from there to demonstrate the dramatic benefits for officials and citizens via privatization of government services.

You will find the volume both a practical guide as well as a helpful instrument in persuading your colleagues and constituencies of the merits of contracting out.

For public officials seeking a breakout from excruciating problems, the chapters prepared by these knowledgeable authors are invaluable.

This way up.

—The Editors,
Raymond Q. Armington
and William D. Ellis

I

MAKING THIS BOOK WORK FOR YOU

For You Personally. For Your Constituency.

by Raymond Q. Armington and William D. Ellis

Privatization Puts into Your Hand the Ancient Power and Efficiency of the Ability to Shop Around.

What This Book Can Do for You

"Look. The commuter types in your ward move out here to Westlake and right away push for stepped-up services," the ash-haired veteran councilman from Ward 1 stabbed a 50-caliber work-blunt finger at his tired young counterpart from Ward 6, "then you vote against us rezoning for light industry to get some tax money to pay for them. Your ward can't have it both ways."

Ward 6 started to answer, but the sunburned city engineer cut in, "Clyde, rezoning will be for nothing until we get sewer money. They're going to freeze new development until we get the sewers in compliance."

There it was again, the twin sharp horns—services and money.

The clock scissored midnight. The mayor said, "We'll wrap it for tonight. We'll talk to the EPA guy tomorrow."

Thinking about what he had heard, Ward 3 councilman, Charles O. "Pete" Thompson, stuffed papers in a hundred-thousand-mile briefcase. He was still thinking about it as he drove his van down his street. He flicked his lights at two neighbors who were walking dogs, knowing they were not thinking about it . . . yet.

"What's he do?" one asked the other.

"Don't know. Something up at City Hall."

That dialogue took place 150 yards from the home of Charles "Pete" Thompson, 1078 Richmar Drive, Westlake, Ohio, a street full of executives. Yet, as a city official, Thompson has a bigger job than most of those neighbors who don't know what he does.

He is expected to deploy prudently more millions of dollars than his usual counterparts in other professions and industries. He needs to be part lawyer, engineer, financier, executive, and environmentalist.

Every local public official is also automatically a public relations person. Whether elected or appointed, he or she is also a legislator or a lobbyist.

This is a crushing load.

Thompson carries it well. But to turn in a high performance in all those functions in a large city, even most superstar local officials need a highly motivated super staff which only exists on Fantasy Island.

However, there is one way an official can create such support. Privatization of services.

This gives the local official choices of the best performance available on the open market. Privatization or contracting out puts in his hands the means to motivate. It gives him the ultimate strength of the shopper.

The companion volume to this, *MORE: The Rediscovery of American Common Sense,* documents that strength in events that you will recognize and by experts whom you will recognize. But *this* handbook spells out the route to that strength in seven specific services named in the table of contents.

For best results from this book, identify yourself as accurately as possible:

— Veteran municipal problem-solver?
— Ambition-driven careerist?
— Dedicated young reformer?

— Politically secure official seeking improvements for the constituency?

— Actively involved citizen?

— Politically besieged official seeking breakthrough solution for financially troubled municipality?

— A new mayor or city manager needing to circumvent entrenched establishment where elected staff is more captive than boss?

— Candidate needing to offer platform of dramatic benefits?

— A mayor trying to get loose from federal money and interference?

— Combination of which of these?

Privatization of services offers the game-breaking play for all these officials.

Why?

It frees them for their main jobs of planning, implementing, instructing, inspecting, and correcting deficiencies. How? By giving them these powerful advantages:

• Guaranteed contract costs
• Flexibility to shop for best performance
• Aggressive program management by contractors competing for contract renewal
• Dramatically improved costs
• Relief from stultifying, complex personnel problems plaguing some in-house departments
• An end-around play in the case of perennially recalcitrant departments staffed by patronage
• Relief from capital costs (fire engines, rubbish trucks, snow plows, and so forth)
• Conversion of *tax-using* functions to *tax-paying* functions.

The Timing is Right

Local governments are being one-two punched across the United States.

The mayor and planning council of a Great Lakes city drag themselves back to the office after supper. The dead-end financial arithmetic on the crumpled yellow sheets among the ashtrays has not improved since this afternoon. At the very time that they are losing revenue from the exodus of a machine tool factory and the big foundry, their unemployed citizens are showing up at council meetings demanding more services.

Down in Texas, a mayor opens the DiGel and attacks the problem: His municipal systems are sinking under the migration from the Great Lakes region. The population outran the planners.

Over in Beautiful Bay, the city manager enters the old city hall by the back door to avoid the sidewalk pedestrians until he solves some of their problems. The city has just been discovered by two regiments of early retirees seeking a pleasant environment and climate where prices have not yet gone city. Services are deluged.

Over in beautiful Orchardville, the council approves the hiring of a financial consultant firm. The lovely, sleepy city has been discovered by waves of "Yumpies" fleeing the suburbs and exurbs, invading the farm country, overburdening all systems.

Local government officials are searching desperately for a life preserver.

Meanwhile, a life preserver sits there . . . available . . . privatization of services, the common sense strategy for breaking out of our problems . . . now.

The time is also right because the first crust of resistance to privatization has been broken. There is now a track record to cite to your colleagues, and opponents, and the media. For example, solid waste collection in more than 60 percent of our communities is now handled by private collectors. Privatization of fire departments is already growing at a compound rate of 30 percent per year. Contract management of waste-water treatment plants is turning in a proven record of cost control and efficient environmental compliance.

Much of the hard pioneering has been done.

Of course that is double-edged. While you no longer have need to introduce privatization from scratch as a new concept, the very success of privatization has alerted the vested opposition—political patronage givers and takers, unions, and municipal employees and their families, and that part of the constituency which sincerely believes that privatization promotes kickback corruption. In overcoming those attitudes, you might find it very helpful to circulate among the leadership the companion volume to this, entitled *MORE*. A first important step would be to see that copies are available in your library.

The time is right also because the quality product syndrome is finally catching on strong. That syndrome transfers to government services. The world resisted the new standards of value (price and quality) established by a small island nation in the Pacific, thinking it would go away, or could be overwhelmed and offset by TV advertising or sloganeering . . . Buy American or Buy Canadian. But the new quality mystique would not go away. The trouble was that the customers liked it.

Industry finally had to realize that Japan was not a gimmick. The manufacturers, therefore, had to demand the new standards from their suppliers. The suppliers, in turn, had to demand them of their vendors. Those vendors, in turn, had to demand more of their components' suppliers. Thus the quality syndrome chainreacted throughout the economy.

In this quality-conscious climate, you now have a much better chance of selling privatization of local government services.

This handbook contains convincing documentation for your use with your constituency, your fellow officials, and council members.

What This Book Can Do for Your Constituents

The Return to Customer Status

Lanky Mayor James H. Cowles, Bay Village, Ohio, strides easily about the big crowd at the annual Kiwanis pancake breakfast. He's wearing a big grin. He gets stopped every two yards by a voter, and he loves it. He feels at home at every podium in town and equally at home in a lumberjack shirt helping the elderly during a snowstorm. He is returned to office repeatedly.

He can afford exposure without fear, because he treats the citizens as customers. He even invites them to see him in his newsletter, "If you have any problems with the services, please stop in and see me or call my office."

And when they call, he is available.

This is in a large suburb of sophisticated upwardly mobile types who could cause plenty of misery. But Mayor Cowles leaves them no room for that.

He has bought them the best services available. They free up his time to inspect, instruct, correct, and mingle with the citizens in order to monitor the results.

Privatization of services puts the citizen back in the position of customer. How? On the one hand, if a contractor for rubbish removal irritates the citizenry with poor service, he can be replaced. On the other hand, if a citizen irritates the *municipal* rubbish collector, he probably gets his rubbish left at the curb, and perhaps the following imperious note:

> Your rubbish container has the
> following violation:
> No handles
> Rubbish collection is a hazardous job,
> endangering the collector. If this vio-
> lation is not corrected, your rubbish
> will not be collected, with the possible
> hazard of a fine for leaving uncollect-
> ed rubbish at the curb.

Under privatization, the citizen is relieved of the frustrating uphill battle of encouraging excellence from some departments grown arrogant from the absence of competition.

Financial Advantage

The most specific boon to the citizen, however, is cost efficiency. This handbook repeatedly documents savings in the range of 30–40 percent, combined with greater efficiency as contractors perform well to earn contract renewal.

The greatest, but least visible benefit to the citizen, is restoring his liberty, his role as the boss, not the servant, of his government. This is probably also the least saleable benefit, as the citizen demonstrates profligate waste of his liberty.

If you are launching a campaign for privatization which you feel requires a strong selling effort in your city, an effective move could be setting up a meeting for the media, building a documented presentation from the examples in this book, showing the dollar improvements achieved by the case examples cited here.

That presentation could be repeated at meetings of the businessmen's lunch club, the main lodges, and other civic organizations where citizen leadership assembles. To assist the media, it might be well to make copies of this book available to them.

The companion volume, *MORE: The Rediscovery of American Common Sense,* is also a persuasive tool in making the financial case for privatization.

Fight This Book

Before using this book with your colleagues and the media and the constituents to launch privatization programs, throw at it all the challenges you would raise as a healthily cynical official.

"Yes, but the authors probably chose ideal communities for their examples."

"Yes, but the authors show only their best cases, not discussing failures."

"Yes, but who put the book together and what ax are they grinding?"

You will find the book meets the knowledgeable cynic head on.

Emphatically, the organization which assembled the chapters is grinding an ax. It is an ax that you can take or leave without diminishing the benefits of privatization, but we had better take a look at that ax in any case.

The Birth of this Book

Down on the Leesburg Pike in Falls Church, Virginia, the famous troop-mobilizing post for the Revolution, began a nonprofit, nonpartisan organization, called the American Society of Local Officials (ASLO). It is also mobilizing a revolution for liberty. ASLO is working to recapture individual liberty by keeping the government at the grass roots level close to the citizens who elect it, fighting federal intrusion.

At this writing, the ASLO chairman is Paul W. Weyrich. He is also executive director of the Committee for the Survival of a Free Congress. The president is Charles E. Thomann. The vice president is Patrick Fagan.

One of the ways ASLO grinds its localization-of-government ax is to help local governments operate free of strings from higher echelons.

The most powerful tool in this effort is the privatization of local government services. Privatization not only increases efficiency but also cuts the cost. It leaves the citizen in charge through his nearby representative, because if he or she does not like the service, it can be shifted to a better private contractor.

The society assists its member officials with privatization of various services. In this work, it has called for the preparation of comprehensive instruction documents for privatization of seven services. These are so useful that the society sought a way to get these distributed *beyond* its own membership to all local officials in the United States. The society got together with Regnery Gateway, Inc., a Chicago publisher with an interest in American history and American government. Regnery Gateway, for example, published the distinguished *Roots of American Order* by Russell Kirk.

Does ASLO staff prepare these advisory materials?

No.

ASLO utilized the expertise of cooperating specialist associations and organizations.

The various associations and their authors will be introduced at the beginning of each chapter. The selected authors are experienced, highly qualified, and active in their separate fields.

The chapters are not philosophical tracts, but working

manuals on how to proceed with specific privatization. Nevertheless, they do such a thorough job of documenting the results of privatization that you will find the chapters useful sales tools in getting the backing of your fellow officials and media and voters for privatization of services.

The Handbook does not need to be read in sequence. Jump to your favorite subject first.

II

TRANSIT SYSTEMS

by Robert W. Poole, Jr.
President, Reason Foundation

Seeming logic: that brief, heavy rush-hour traffic should capture the most profit for a transit system.

Seeming logic: a single, integrated city-transit system should be more efficient than a hodgepodge of various systems competing side-by-side.

Seeming logic: for the most fiscal efficiency—larger vehicles, fewer stops.

Seeming logic: the way to hold down fares for commuters is via public subsidized transit.

No.

Analyst Robert Poole documents in this chapter how apparant logic in transit can lead us 180 degrees wrong. He shows that rush hours contribute most to transit company *deficits*; a hodgepodge of modes competing side-by-side in apparent confusion actually delivers an amazingly systematic, dependable service; and a large number of small vehicles is probably more efficient than the opposite.

These are only a few of the folk-wisdoms that Poole overturns with solid documentation. His is an extremely useful analysis.

Poole specifically does *not* fault the managers of government subsidized systems. The pressure is on them to seek and accept government subsidies. However, once they have accepted, the finest of managers cannot win. The subsidy carries the genes of failure. It immediately promotes inefficiencies, requiring more subsidies, in turn, promoting more inefficiencies; the self-feeding spiral crashes in transit disaster.

Robert Poole, with bachelor's and master's degrees from Massachusetts Institute of Technology (M.I.T.), has been involved in local government studies during his entire professional life, with the exception of three years as a systems analyst for Sikorsky Aircraft. He was co-founder of the Local Government Center, a consulting and research organization counseling local governments. This group was absorbed by The Reason Foundation. Before that Poole worked seven years with local governments in nine states.

His chapter is a lucid analysis, richly documented with real success stories, providing positive recommendations for transit success. The reader cannot help but find multiple solutions to seemingly insoluble problems in this comprehensive chapter, a rare compendium, indeed, of the best transit results in the world.

You will find this chapter also valuable in reminding your colleagues and city councilmen and administrators and voters that we have more choices than we are regularly considering. Poole explains the advantages of using transit contract managers. He reminds us of the alternatives, the possiblity of paratransit services, jitney services, private subscription transport, vanpooling, and transit brokerage.

In showing proof of the market and profitability of these other systems, often made illegal by old restrictive regulations, Poole points to the voluminous and successful black market using plain painted sedans. If anyone asks, "This is just a car pool." But those *for-hire* car pools provide excellent service at good rates, demonstrating the viability of the market.

Finally, Poole points out that in the depths of a city's despair about its transit mess, there is one move a city can make that will almost overnight bring enormous relief to overburdened transit systems. Remove from the books restrictions on private operators.

At the close of the chapter, Poole cites an outstanding approach made by Knoxville, Tennessee, which may offer a perfect route for your city.

If you are leading a movement in your city for improving the transit system and have several meetings with leadership and media planned, you will find this chapter an effective outline for your presentation, localizing the examples, where appropriate.

For bolstering your case with certain of your most vigorous but sincere and analytical opponents, you will find in Poole's list of references strong support materials.

If you have in your city a thoughtful, influential transporation journalist, it would be well to loan him this chapter ... along with a copy of *MORE*, the companion to this volume.

One of the least productive things we do in this country is move millions of people back and forth to their jobs every day. Any improvement in passenger hours thus spent has a multiplier of millions.

—The Editors

Mass transit is an essential component of an urban area's transportation system. Although automobiles are the overwhelming choice of most commuters and metropolitan area residents, increasing traffic congestion motivates many commuters to leave the driving to someone else. In addition, some people are either unable or unwilling to drive. Thus, transportation services for hire are necessary and important.

Today, most urban mass transit is provided or controlled by government agencies. The typical pattern is a two-tier system, with low-fare (but heavily subsidized) bus service provided by the city government or a regional transit agency and high-fare (unsubsidized) taxicab service provided by franchised private companies. In a handful of very large cities, there is also a commuter rail system, and this, too, is government-operated and heavily subsidized.

From a financial standpoint, municipal transit systems are a disaster. Whereas farebox revenues covered 92 percent of transit operating costs in 1965, they covered only 38 percent by 1980, as federal state, and local subsidies proliferated. Table 1 shows where nine fairly typical municipal transit systems obtain their revenues. As can be seen, taxpayer subsidies predominate, especially in larger cities.

TABLE 1
Transit System Revenue Sources for Selected Cities

Large Cities	Farebox Percentage	Percent of Subsidies		
		Federal	State	Local
MBTA—Boston*	22%	9%	41%	28%
MTA—Houston*	18	23	8	51
SCCT—San Jose*	9	6	30	55
BART—San Francisco†	25	2	9	64
SCRTD—Los Angeles*	39	16	45	0
Average	23%	11%	27%	40%
Small Cities				
ConnDOT—Hartford*	46	27	27	0
Pentran—Newport News*	35	32	3	30
Tidewater—Norfolk*	45	29	5	21
SRT—Sacramento†	25	27	42	6
Average	38%	29%	19%	14%

*Roger F. Teal, Genevieve Giuliano, and Mary E. Brenner, "Transit Agency Use of Private Sector Strategies for Commuter Transportation," Institute of Transportation Studies, Irvine: University of California, January 1983.

†"California Transit Systems," *Cal-Tax Research Bulletin*, Sacramento, January 15-31, 1981.

This dependence on subsidies should be cause for concern, for at least two reasons. First, although transit system ridership continues its historic decline (transit systems carried 9 percent of all commuters in 1970 but only 6.4 percent in 1980—a 2.9-percent decrease)[1], transit subsidies continue to increase. *The reason for the increase is the tendency of subsidies to promote economically inefficient practices.* For example, of the 148-percent increase in transit operating costs between 1967 and 1976, more than two-thirds of the increase (actually 71 percent) was absorbed into higher wages and a larger white-collar labor force, rather than to fund expanded service.[2] Above-market wages, restrictive work-rule practices (e.g., restrictions or bans on part-time drivers), and a refusal to drop poorly utilized routes are examples of inefficiencies encouraged by heavy subsidization.

Second, long-term continuation of these subsidies cannot be assumed. In 1981, the Reagan administration announced its intention to phase out federal operating subsidies for mass transit within three years. Although Congress has not gone that far, future Congresses—faced with continued huge deficits—might well do so. Moreover, state and local tax-limitation measures threaten the continued growth, if not the existence, of state and local transit subsidies. As transit ridership continues to decline, fewer and fewer voters will perceive any direct benefit in being taxed to provide transit systems.

The effect of a federal aid phase-out would be more severe in smaller cities. Nationwide, federal subsidies accounted for only 18 percent of the average transit operating budget in cities over one million people, but 33 percent of the budget for cities under 250,000[3]—results that parallel those shown in Table 1. In addition, cities over one million tend to have higher densities and a more transit-dependent population. Thus, their transit systems are in a better position to raise fares to make up for lost subsidy revenue without driving away riders. (Large cities have what economists call a lower "elasticity of demand" for transit—i.e., people are less likely to stop riding due to transit price increases.) Thus, it is the hundreds of smaller cities—not the cities of a million or more people—whose transit systems could be devastated by a federal aid phase-out.[4]

Whence the Problem?

To correct the problem, we need to know its sources.

The underlying cause of municipal transit systems' huge losses is the same as that which led to the failure of their private-enterprise predecessors: suburbanization.

Following World War II, America's urban areas underwent an unprecedented decentralization, aided by federal policy in the form of FHA and VA mortgages, mortgage-interest deductibility, and federally subsidized urban expressway construction. The drastically reduced density changed the economics of fixed-route mass transit. Bus companies lost much of their market in the urban core and found it much more expensive to serve a widely dispersed suburban population, most of whom preferred automobiles in any event. And state and/or local regulatory policies generally made it difficult for the franchised bus companies to raise rates, or adopt distance-based fares, or drop lines with low ridership. The result, predictably enough, was bankruptcy for most local bus firms.

The flood of red ink and bankruptcies constituted important, but unheeded, economic information. The message was that the existing form of transit system—grid-type, fixed-route service—was no longer economically viable. Some new form of transit was needed to meet the needs of a decentralized market. But instead of heeding this message, civic leaders determined to preserve the obsolete form of mass transit by having local government "nationalize" the failing bus companies (and occasional rail lines).

Because the bus companies generally failed to invest in new equipment or adequate maintenance during their final, loss-plagued years of existence, the initial hope of local transit officials was that a one-time infusion of capital to refurbish the transit systems would attract new riders and put the systems back in the black. This was the rationale behind the Urban Mass Transportation Act of 1964, which set up a program of federal grants for capital equipment. But since old equipment was not the real problem, transit ridership continued to drop, and transit system losses continued to mount. That, in turn, led to pressure for further federal subsidies, culminating in the Urban Mass Transportation Act of 1974, which provided for *operating* subsidies, in addition to capital grants. Yet as we have seen, transit ridership has continued its long, steady decline.

Ironically, the deficit caused by the reality of failing urban transit situations has been exacerbated by the operating policies of many municipal transit agencies. Most municipal transit today is heavily oriented around peak-hour service. Two-thirds of all transit trips occur during four hours per day, five days per week, of morning and evening rush hours.[5] Since transit operators buy enough vehicles and hire enough drivers to handle these peak loads, most of the vehicles and labor are underutilized the majority of the time.

In fact, a number of recent studies has shown that the cost of adding additional capacity to handle peak-load demands is far greater than the extra revenue the extra capacity produces. Thus, off-peak transit service comes closer to covering its costs than peak-load service.[6] Transit economists are now generally agreed that peak-hour service produces a disproportionate share of the transit deficit, and that *the key to cutting the system's deficit is to "shed" peak-period service to lower-cost providers.*

Unfortunately, few transit agency managers have come to this realization, as yet. Generally, they view the peak-load periods as their basic source of *revenue*, rather than as their basic source of *deficits*. Thus, they adamantly oppose allowing any other providers to offer competing services during peak hours, arguing that such services will "skim the cream" off their revenues. But shedding load during peak periods is far more likely to result in skimming off *deficits*, thereby improving the transit systems' financial health.[7]

Solving the Transit Problem

What can be done to provide better mass transit at less cost to the taxpayers? We have seen that today's fixed-route, government-operated systems are a poor match for the decentralized, suburban nature of most metropolitan areas. But what kind of mass transit would make sense?

Economists and social scientists have conducted numerous studies of transportation preferences. Automobiles are the choice for most people because they offer speed, flexibility (both as to time and destination), comfort, safety, and privacy —at a cost most people perceive as reasonable. Conventional city buses, by contrast, are slow, are not door-to-door (requiring of commuters long waiting and walking times to and from bus stops), inflexible (serving only a limited number of fixed routes), less comfortable than cars, and much less private. Thus, the low out-of-pocket cost must be weighed against a long list of disadvantages.

Door-to-Door Travel Time

By far the most important attribute of a transit system is door-to-door travel time.[8] Even gleaming, new subway lines have failed to attract the anticipated level of ridership, despite huge subsidies that hold down fares to a fraction of actual cost. Low levels of ridership persist because high operating speed does not compensate for the long waits at stations or the long walks required to get to and from stations. Rail system stations *must* be widely spaced in order to permit high-speed operation between stations. Thus, any proposed transit alternative should focus on reduced travel time.

Large Vehicle/Small Vehicle

Unfortunately, the trend in today's municipal transit systems is toward longer and longer travel times. Over the past decade, system operators have been shifting to larger and larger vehicles—forsaking vans and minibuses for conventional 50- to 60-seat buses and even adding huge 70-seat articulated buses. The principal reason for the shift to ever-larger vehicles is the above-market wages paid to bus drivers, resulting from the superior bargaining position of transit unions in dealing with a monopoly provider of mass transit. With drivers often making $30,000 or more per year, a transit agency's incentive is to get as much out of each driver as possible—i.e., to have them drive 70-seat articulated buses, rather than a 20-seat minibus.

But from the standpoint of the passenger, the move to larger vehicles is a step in the wrong direction. If the 600 daily seats on a given route are parceled out in 20-seat minibuses, 30 vehicles will be available. But if those same 600 seats are provided by 60-seat buses, only 10 vehicles will be available to service the route. The frequency of service will obviously be three times greater with a 30-vehicle fleet than with 10 vehicles—and the average passenger waiting time at the bus stop correspondingly lower. Thus, we can see how the high cost of drivers has led transit agencies to provide the wrong kind of vehicles—if door-to-door speed (which attracts riders) is to be emphasized. It is little wonder that transit ridership continues to decline as the average vehicle size increases.

Flexibility

Besides higher door-to-door speed, an improved mass transit system must provide greater *flexibility*, if it is to succeed in competing with autos in serving decentralized metropolitan areas. But as Gabriel Roth and George Wynne point out, "[S]uburban living cannot be efficiently served by fixed-route bus or rail lines: fast door-to-door service in low-density neighborhoods can only be provided by a transport made flexible enough to arrive quickly close to people's homes in response to their need."[9] This suggests that at least a significant component of urban transportation must be provided by decentralized, demand-responsive forms of transportation rather than fixed-route bus lines.

Cost

In addition to speed and flexibility, *cost* is also a consideration. All too often, the cost of a municipal transit system is taken as an irreducible minimum. It is assumed that any other form of transit would have to cost more, if it provided a higher level of service (e.g., fewer seats, no standees, door-to-door operation) or if private, or if it had to make a profit.

This seemingly plausible view overlooks the relationship between costs and incentives. A government-run mass transit system is operated as a virtual monopoly and has ready access to taxpayer-supplied subsidies. The absence of competition and the presence of subsidies provide few meaningful incentives for efficient, cost-conscious operation. Thus, for example, employee wages can be bid up to levels far above what would prevail in a competitive market. Token sellers on the New York subway, for example, were being paid $21,888 per year in 1978, while intermediate-level bank tellers in New York—a job requiring considerably higher skill levels—were earning only $11,767.[10] Foolish work rules, such as restrictions or outright bans on part-time drivers, can be forced on transit management by a monopolistic union. Lightly patronized routes can be kept in operation year after year due to political pressures. All of these inefficiencies stem directly from the institutional structure of a transit system as a subsidized monopoly. None of them is inherent in the nature of urban mass transportation.

Two examples serve to illustrate that transit costs are not simply "given." When Chicago's Regional Transportation Authority (RTA) increased transit fares sharply in 1981–82, hundreds of groups of commuters got together and organized bus pools, chartering buses from commercial bus companies. As of early 1982, many of these commuters were paying between $39 and $52 per month, which covered all costs of the operation.[11] For those same commuters, their average RTA fare had been $80 per month—and that charge only covered about *half* of RTA's costs. Thus, ordinary Chicago-area commuters, with no knowledge of transportation planning, were able to figure out how to provide commuter service for less than *one-third* the cost of the local transit agency.

In 1982, the Southern California Association of Governments conducted a study of the express bus service being provided by the Southern California Rapid Transit District (SCRTD). Though popular with commuters, the service turned out to be much more costly than SCRTD's regular bus service. When the analysts compared the express service with that operated by private-subscription bus companies, they found that the private firms' costs were *half* those of the subsidized public system.[12] Turning over the operation of express bus service to the private sector could save the taxpayers $4.6 million a year, the study concluded.

It should be clear from the foregoing that the solution to urban transit problems does not lie in further subsidizing an inefficient, monopolistic fixed-route system. *Real hope for improved transit lies with introducing decentralized, flexible, private transportation alternatives.*

Evidence from Abroad

Are there any cities where decentralized, flexible, private transportation exists? In the United States, for the most part, the answer is no. As noted earlier, transit agency managements generally take the view that competition from the private sector is a threat to their revenues, rather than a means of reducing their deficits. Thus, except for a legally restricted amount of premium-priced taxicab service, most other forms of private transit are simply not allowed. That includes commercial (for-hire) car-pools, van-pools, and bus-pools as well as jitneys (van-type vehicles operating on semi-fixed routes), and private bus services.

But in major cities overseas—especially in South America and Southeast Asia—private transit is often allowed to operate side-by-side with public transit. World Bank transportation economist Gabriel Roth has spent years studying these systems and is convinced they offer many lessons for American cities, as well.[13]

Buenos Aires

An excellent example is Buenos Aires, the capital of Argentina, a city of 9 million people spread out over 1,500 square miles. Aside from a relatively old subway system, all mass transit in the city is provided by private buses called "collectivos"—most of them 23-seat minibuses. Altogether there are 13,000 of these buses in service, providing 75 percent of all public transport trips. It is interesting to note that when the government dissolved its money-losing transit monopoly in 1962, much of the vehicle fleet sold off to private operators consisted of full-size buses. But given a free hand, nearly all the route associations (called "Empresas") have replaced the large vehicles with minibuses, which provide more frequent service and lower unit costs. Needless to say, the Empresas receive no government subsidy and for the most part make profits for their owners.

Calcutta

A much denser city is Calcutta, India, home to 10 million mostly poor people. Time is not of such high value to them and India's climate and culture do not promote hustle and bustle. Thus, it is not surprising to find large buses predominating in Calcutta. What *is* surprising is the presence of 2,000 private buses (1,500 full-size, 500 minibuses) operating in competition with an equivalent number of buses of the

Calcutta State Transport Corporation (CSTC). Although CSTC has kept the best routes for itself, the private operators manage to carry *two-thirds* of all bus trips in Calcutta. Moreover, they do so without subsidy, while CSTC loses some $12 million a year. Yet both bus systems charge identical fares. Clearly, the private operators have learned how to operate at much lower cost. Their labor productivity is far higher than CSTC's (which employs 30 people per bus). They have negligible "fare evasion" (compared with 25 percent on CSTC buses) because the private bus drivers receive a percentage of revenues. And they keep their vehicles in good repair by using local garages, in contrast with CSTC's bureaucratic maintenance procedures (which result in only about half of its buses being in service in any time).

Hong Kong

Nearly as dense as Calcutta is the city of Hong Kong, whose five million people are crowded into 400 square miles. Besides a (privately owned but subsidized) subway line and several franchised bus lines, Hong Kong's largely private transit system includes 4,350 minibuses, 328 "maxicabs," and some 10,000 taxicabs. The minibuses—whose number has now been frozen by the government—operate along busy streets but do not follow fixed routes, per se, thereby having some of the characteristics of jitneys. Their fares are not regulated, and they generally fluctuate, increasing during peak hours when demand is high and decreasing during slack time to attract business. Many of the minibuses are owner-operated. The maxicabs are government-run minibuses which operate on fixed routes, at prices based on mileage but not on time of day. Additional taxi licenses are auctioned off annually by the government, at the rate of 1,200 per year. Demand for taxi service is so high--despite the expanding supply--that the licenses go for as much as $50,000.

Manila

Yet another city with largely private transit is Manila, capital of the Philippines. While buses provide 25 percent of all trips and automobiles (including taxis) another 25 percent, one-half of all trips occur in a uniquely Filipino form of jitney--the Jeepney. Originally constructed from surplus U.S. Army jeeps, today's Jeepneys are manufactured locally. With an extended chassis, lengthwise upholstered benches, and fringed roof, the 14-passenger, gaudily painted vehicles make a unique contribution to the city's ambience as well as to its transportation system. World Bank cost analyses estimate that a 14-seat jitney's operating cost is about one-fourth that of a 58-seat bus, making the two modes' cost-per-seat-mile roughly comparable. (A 1979 study gave a Jeepney cost of 40 cents per-seat-mile while the bus operating cost was 46.5 cents per-seat-mile.[14])

Others

Numerous other examples of private transit overseas exist—minibuses in Bangkok, Istanbul, and Kuala Lumpur; taxis and jitneys in Cairo; vans and minibuses in Nairobi and Khartoum; shared taxis in Belfast and Caracas; and so forth. Closer to home, Puerto Rico has for 25 years permitted jitneys (known as "Publicos") to compete with government-run bus systems. A recent study of jitney service in Caguas by the Puerto Rico Department of Transportation[15] found that in 1980 the Publicos carried five-sixths of all trips, and did so at a profit, charging a 50-cent fare. The city bus system, by contrast, served one-sixth of the riders, and covered only 35 percent of its costs, charging 25 cents. The report concluded that the Publico system was financially and economically viable, while the bus system could only be made viable by a shift to minibuses.

Common Denominators of Success

Roth and Wynne assessed these and other private-transit success stories, so as to isolate their most important characteristics. Their conclusions were as follows:

   • *Private ownership.* It is the inability of private owners to obtain subsidies and their ability to drop or avoid lightly patronized routes that keep their operating costs low.

- *Small vehicles.* Besides improved passenger service (shorter waiting time, fewer stops), smaller vehicles cost less *per seat* to purchase (because they are mass-produced) and to operate, and are easier to maneuver in traffic. Nonsubsidized transit operators facing competition nearly always choose minibuses.
- *Small operating units.* There are very few economies of scale in urban transit. Hence, small firms can be viable competitors. Moreover, the small-business owner is generally far more cost-conscious and willing to work much harder to make a success of the business than a hired manager. Transit needs can be provided as well or better by numerous small firms as opposed to one large agency.
- *Route associations.* A common device to organize small-scale operators is the route association, in which owner-drivers band together to provide service on a particular route, generally charging a common fare. In some cities, route associations succeed in monopolizing service on particular routes, while in others (including Buenos Aires, Hong Kong, and Manila) competing route associations are common.

Applying the Lessons

How can American cities apply the lessons from abroad to solve their urban transit problems? Remembering the earlier discussion about (a) the need for reducing the load on the system at peak hours; and (b) the need for flexible, decentralized service in suburban areas, the basic solution is for transit agencies to encourage, rather than discourage, the introduction of private transit services. Private alternatives can take over a portion of the peak-hour load, thereby enabling the transit agency to reduce costly overstaffing and overequipping, *and* can substitute for transit agency buses in low-density areas where smaller vehicles and more flexible service are clearly preferable.

There are three basic tools that local governments can use to restructure and revitalize urban transit. These tools are (1) contracting out; (2) deregulation; and (3) transit brokerage. Each will be explained in the paragraphs which follow.

1. Contracting Out. As we have seen, one way to reduce the transit agency's deficit is by reducing services at peak periods, thereby permitting the gradual reduction of excessive equipment and personnel. A second way to reduce losses is to replace large, agency-operated buses on low-ridership suburban routes with lower-cost small vehicles operated by private firms. Both types of service can be—and are being—contracted out.

A good example of peak-hour transit agency contracting is the "club bus" program of Golden Gate Transit District in San Francisco. Since the early 1970s, this agency has been contracting with private bus companies to provide express service for commuters. As of 1982, there were four companies involved, providing 27 bus runs each morning and afternoon rush hours. Each bus serves a "commute club" of mostly white-collar workers who live in Marin and Sonoma counties, north of San Francisco. Each club determines the schedule and pickup points, collects dues, and makes a monthly payment to the district. The latter contracts for buses and drivers from charter bus companies, on a competitive bidding basis.

This type of express-bus contracting is not unique to the San Francisco area. Houston's MTA contracts for 13 express bus routes, although that agency views contracting as only a temporary expedient, its management apparently not perceiving the loss-producing nature of the peak-load problem. By contrast, transit agency managements of Hartford's Conn-DOT, Newport News's Pentran, and Norfolk's Tidewater Transportation District (as well as Golden Gate Transit District) "all perceive the peak period as a major source of deficits," according to a recent study by transit economists Teal, Guiliano, and Brenner of the University of California's Institute of Transportation Studies.[16]

Thus, all four agencies contract with private sector operators for peak-period service. In Hartford, ConnDOT contracts for service with six companies on six different routes, on a subsidized basis. Pentran and Tidewater follow a somewhat different model, purchasing both full-size and mini-buses and leasing them out to private firms to operate. No direct subsidies are involved, but the companies avoid the up-front capital requirements and benefit from lower leasing costs, due to the government status of the agencies, which permits them to obtain buses via grants and tax-exempt bonds.

Replacing large, high-cost buses with small, low-cost paratransit vehicles to serve low-density routes is another strategy that is beginning to gain acceptance. Norfolk's Tidewater Transportation District is an excellent case in point. For several years, it has contracted with taxicab firms to take over service on lightly patronized bus routes, both in low-density suburbs and during evening hours. Cab companies bid competitively on the basis of qualifications and cost per vehicle hour. The service offered on these routes is door-to-door, "demand-responsive"—i.e., on the same level as regular taxi service. Yet the net cost to the district ends up being lower than the previous bus service.[17]

Several other cities are also substituting vans or taxis for money-losing bus routes. Phoenix, Arizona, contracts with local taxi companies to provide service on its bus routes on Sundays, when ridership is but a small fraction of what it is during the rest of the week. Arabi, Louisiana; Chapel Hill, North Carolina; and Westport, Connecticut, all contract with taxi companies for regular daily transit service. In Westport, there was no public transit prior to 1974, when a paratransit-oriented agency was created, using a fleet of minibuses. In 1977, the agency leased 11 vans to a newly formed taxi company, to be operated in coordination with the agency's own minibuses. During peak periods, the vans supplement the agency's commuter routes; during off-peak hours, the vans provide shared dial-a-ride service.[18]

San Diego Transit Corporation (a municipal bus agency, despite its name), in 1982 went out to bid for paratransit service for its Paradise Hills suburb, to provide fixed-route, peak-period service and dial-a-ride off-peak service using small vehicles. Roth reports that more than 50 community transit services are operated by taxi companies under contract in California alone.[19] A number of other taxi-substitution projects are described in the 1976 Urban Institute report.[20]

Kenneth Orski reports that contracting out low-demand

service to taxi companies is occurring overseas as well. Karls-
ruhe, Munich, Stuttgart, and West Berlin are among the cities
that are contracting for fixed-route, scheduled taxi service
instead of buses at night, at significant cost savings.[21] In
Canada, Regina, Saskatchewan's Telebus project has substi-
tuted a van-based dial-a-ride service in its low-density suburbs
for conventional bus service. Subsidies have been cut by 25
percent while ridership has actually increased 14 percent,
thanks to improved service.[22]

A third type of contracting out also offers the potential for
cost savings: hiring a transit management firm to operate the
municipal bus system. The largest firm in the field,
Cincinnati-based ATE Management and Service Co., has
management contracts with 51 municipal transit agencies in
this country, including Charlotte, Cincinnati, Sacramento,
and Wilmington. It also operates seven transit systems in
Saudi Arabia. A smaller rival firm, American Transit Corporation of St. Louis, manages 16 systems under contract.

Transit management contractors can save money for several reasons. First of all, they can benefit from economies of
scale, using such techniques as bulk purchasing, self-
insurance, shared-use of computer software, rather than
scaling all of the operation to the dimensions of a single
agency. Second, because they must compete periodically for
the contract, private firms have stronger incentives to be
aggressive in seeking operating efficiencies, as has been
observed in numerous other areas of contracting out public
services. Their employees may be better motivated, too—for
example, ATE employees participate in a profit-sharing plan.

Public services consultant James L. Mercer reports that
ATE has documented impressive cost savings in its various
contract operations—$150,000 a year in one system thanks to
implementation of self-insurance, $200,000 through reduc-
tion in inventory, $170,000 via route rescheduling (with no
cut in service), and $200,000 in operating costs, while revers-
ing a five percent annual ridership loss.[23] More than 90
percent of ATE's contracts have been renewed, since it began
operations in 1969.

Another way in which management contractors can save
money is by restructuring the transit system, along the lines

discussed in this chapter. Some of the cost-saving activities of the Tidewater Transportation District were in fact suggested by ATE while under contract to the district. Private firms are more likely to be receptive to structural changes such as substituting paratransit operators for loss-plagued bus routes. In addition, a private management firm may be more willing to negotiate in a hard-nosed fashion with transit unions over service and work-rule changes.

This brings up the most significant impediment to contracting out: the "labor protection" provision of the Urban Mass Transportation Act, Section 13(c). This provision states that one condition of receipt of federal transit subsidies is that no such agency may take any action that harms existing transit agency workers. Thus, as long as transit agencies accept federal subsidies—and as long as Section 13(c) remains unaltered by Congress—no agency may eliminate employees as a direct result of contracting out service to private operators.[24]

Determining whether a substitution of service causes a *direct* reduction in agency jobs is, however, a matter of interpretation. The Tidewater Transportation District substitued paratransit services for a number of bus routes whose costs were increasing and whose ridership was decreasing. The District's position was that bus service on those routes would have had to be discontinued unless a cheaper substitute was implemented. Despite the fact that no layoffs of district employees resulted from substitution (the district presumably hoped to reduce staffing by attrition, so as to realize the needed cost savings), the transit union has filed suit, alleging violation of provisions of Section 13(c).[25]

It should be noted that the specific provisions implementing 13(c) in a transit agency are negotiated between the agency and the union. Thus, they are not immutable but are subject to revision each time the union contract is up for renewal. Economist Simon Rottenberg has pointed out that agencies have considerable discretion in interpreting the requirements of 13(c) and, in the past, have generally agreed far too readily with the transit unions' very restrictive views. Creative negotiation of this issue could provide a great deal more flexibility for most transit agencies to contract out services, perhaps subject to no-layoff agreements, pending elimination or modification of Section 13(c) by Congress.

2. Deregulation. Besides contracting directly with private transit operators, another alternative is to facilitate their entry or expansion in the local transit market. To the extent that substitute service can be provided by private operators winning away business from the transit agency, no 13(c) complications arise. Yet the entry or expansion of private service is significantly restricted in most cities by state and/or local regulations.

A most important milestone for private transit occurred in October 1982. The Urban Mass Transportation Administraton (UMTA) issued its long-awaited paratransit policy statement. In a speech at the annual convention of the International Taxicab Association, UMTA administrator Arthur Teele, Jr. urged local authorities to join UMTA in promoting paratransit services in a free-market environment as a way of reducing the "mushrooming operating deficits" of local transit systems. Thus, UMTA has given its endorsement to efforts to remove legal and institutional barriers to private transit—to create a free market.

What are those barriers? If a company or individual wants to operate a vehicle for hire, it must first pass muster with local officials. In most cities, anti-jitney laws flatly prohibit the operation of for-hire vehicles except as taxicabs—and in that case, an operating license must be obtained. In most cities, the numer of licenses has long been frozen, so unless an existing operator goes out of business or is willing to sell a license, the would-be applicant is out of luck. Even if he can obtain a license, the amount of service he can provide and the conditions of doing so are spelled out in great detail—and these conditions may often prove financially prohibitive (e.g., a requirement for 24-hour service, which a large cab company could meet by keeping one cab in service all night despite the lack of business, would be ridiculously expensive for a single-cab company). And, of course, the rates will be regulated, meaning the would-be operator cannot be sure of being able to set prices high enough to provide adequate revenues. In some states, instead of, or in addition to, these local hurdles, a would-be operator must go before a state public utilities commission and prove that there is a need for additional service. The way this requirement is usually interpreted, the applicant has the full burden of proof to show that existing operators are inadequate. Generally, as long as the incumbents can show that they are operating responsibly and have the ability to expand to meet any additional demand, the applicant is out of luck.

This dismal picture has begun to change. Here and there enlightened city councils, transit agencies, and state legislators are recognizing the nature of the peak-hour problem and the value of private-transit services. Noting the success of airline and truck deregulation at making more service available at lower average prices, they have begun deregulating local transit, moving toward the free market now advocated by UMTA.

For many years Washington, D.C., was the only major city to permit open entry into the taxicab business. As a result, taxi service in Washington is approximately 10 times as plentiful (on a taxis per thousand population basis) as in other major American cities—over 10 cabs per thousand compared to an average of one cab per thousand in restricted-entry cities.[26] Thus, Washington's experience disproves the contention of taxi-cartel advocates that existing levels of supply are adequate to meet all demand. What the demand will be depends upon the relative scarcity or abundance of taxi service. If only a small number of cabs is allowed, the drivers will concentrate on airport to hotel service, leaving other needs poorly served. By contrast, in Washington cabs are available, cruising the streets throughout the city. Consequently, people have learned that they can depend on cabs as a low-cost, flexible means of transportation.

Over the last five years, a handful of cities has begun deregulating their taxi systems. Both San Diego and Seattle opened up taxicab entry in 1979 and removed all rate regulation within the next year. Other cities that have opened up include Spokane, Honolulu and Santa Barbara (both in 1982 due to concern over possible antitrust liability) and all of Arizona's cities (thanks to the implementation of a statewide transportation deregulation measure in mid-1982).

While it is too early to assess the results in most of these cities, the initial results in San Diego and Seattle have been reviewed in UMTA-funded studies.[27] In San Diego, "the regulatory changes produced a dramatic increase in the size of the local taxi industry." The number of cabs nearly doubled, while the number of firms tripled. Passenger waits at active cab stands have virtually disappeared and response time to telephone requests for service has improved. While fares went up in nominal terms, the increase barely kept pace with the increase in the Consumer Price Index—in other words, *real* fare levels have not increased. In Seattle, the number of cabs increased by 25 percent and the number of companies by 50 percent. The number of licenses held in small companies more than doubled, while that in large service companies remained more or less the same. Fare levels went up only slightly more than the Consumer Price Increase, with the greatest jump in the first quarter following deregulation, indicating that regulation had been holding fares artificially low.

Several other cities have deregulated taxi fares recently, including Eugene, Oregon (1978), Phoenix and Tucson, Arizona (1982), and Kansas City, Missouri (1983). The only significant problem with unregulated fares has occurred at the city airports. Since cabs line up and take passengers on a first-come, first-served basis, some travelers have complained about not getting the lowest-priced cab. In addition, tourists tend to be unfamiliar with the situation and sometimes feel taken advantage of, while local residents realize that it is possible to bargain with the cab drivers for a lower-than-posted fare. These problems have led to calls for some form of controls on airport fares in those cities.

Another way in which taxis can become a more important factor in local transit is if they can be used on a shared-ride basis, i.e., by several passengers going to different destinations. Shared cab riding has long been legal in Washington, D.C. In recent years some forms of shared-ride service—generally at lower fares than for exclusive service—have been legalized in Chicago, Indianapolis, Los Angeles, Miami, Minneapolis, Pittsburgh, Portland, as well as in a number of smaller cities. Kenneth Heathington studied shared-ride service in Davenport, Iowa and Hicksville, Long Island.[28] Both provide door-to-door service at fares about twice that of local bus systems—without subsidy. And both have mass ridership approaching the magnitude of a bus system's. The Hicksville system operates primarily to bring commuters to stations of the Long Island Railroad's commuter trains.

Another very useful form of low-cost paratransit is jitney service. The original jitneys of 1914-22 were mostly modified Model T Fords. So successful were they in competing with streetcar lines—operating along the same general route but with greater frequency and with occasional off-route stops a few blocks on either side of the line—that the streetcar companies succeeded in getting anti-jitney laws enacted in virtually every major American city.[29] Only isolated examples of the original jitneys remain in operation, grandfathered into the restrictive ordinances: along Pacific Avenue in Atlantic City, on Mission and Third Streets in San Francisco, and in the black sections of Baton Rouge and Miami. An 85-vehicle jitney system, the Service Cars, existed in the black neighborhoods of St. Louis until 1965, when state regulators abruptly shut it down.

Despite the laws, however, thriving black-market jitney operations exist in a number of cities, using regular automobiles, limousines, or vans. About 85 jitneys operate in Chattanooga. Hundreds serve the black areas of Pittsburgh, by some accounts outnumbering the legal cabs. Some parallel the bus routes but will make several-block deviation. Others operate essentially as carpools, picking up the same passengers each day. Between 50 and 100 unlicensed limousines operate as jitneys in San Francisco. And over 1,000 "gypsy cabs" serve mostly minority neighborhoods in New York City.[30]

Over the past few years, *legal* jitneys have begun to make a comeback. In Indianapolis, the city approved the local Yellow Cab's application to operate seven 14-passenger jitney vans in 1982. The service was approved over the strong objections of the local transit agency, which opposed the service as "skimming the cream" off its peak-hour business (!). San Diego began permitting jitney service in 1979, when it deregulated cabs. As of 1983, there were 36 jitneys in service, operated by 12 companies. The jitneys transport passengers on shopping trips, to and from the airport and hotels, to and from five local military bases, and to such nearby destinations as La Jolla and Tijuana. Jitney companies can serve any route they choose, except for a congested ¾-mile downtown corridor and routes identical to city bus routes. They are also free to charge whatever the market will bear. Actual fares range from $1.50 to $6.00, depending on route and mileage, compared to 80 cents on the heavily subsidized city buses.

Private bus companies still exist in many urban areas, often operating mostly on a charter basis. In a growing number of cities, charter bus companies have provided the basis for subscription bus services, organized by groups of commuters. In some states, including California, such services must receive a license from the state public utilities commission. This has led to the creation of for-profit companies, such as Southern California's Com-Bus, which serve as intermediaries between groups of commuters and charter bus companies and run interference with the regulators. Com-Bus conducts employee demand surveys, establishes routes and schedules, hires the buses with professional drivers, selects a route coordinator for each bus to collect fares and manage its operations, and obtains the necessary permit from the Public Utilities Commission. As of 1982, there were more than 100 private subscription buses in operation in the Los Angeles metropolitan area. Their operating costs averaged 50 percent less than those of comparable public-sector express bus service.

A similar picture exists in several other major urban areas. Some 600 private express buses serve Manhattan from suburbs in New York state and another 500 from New Jersey. Most of these operations are not subsidized. Numerous subscription buses serve Washington, D.C., from its Maryland and Virginia suburbs. Statistics collected by UMTA indicate that in the 15 largest metropolitan areas, about 15 percent of the buses operating in public transportation are privately operated today.[31] And this is *despite* the restrictive nature of state and local licensing laws. In an open market, the extent of privately operated bus service would undoubtedly be much greater, especially given the large rise in transit agency costs and fares of the past decade.

One state that retains an active private bus industry is New Jersey. About 40 percent of its municipal and intercity buses are privately owned, mostly by small companies (often with owner-drivers). Many of these small firms have coordinated their operations by means of route associations, much like those of Buenos Aires and other cities abroad. On average, these private, unsubsidized firms have fare levels 10 percent lower than state-owned New Jersey Transit buses.[32] The latter loses $50 million a year and frequently protests license applications by the private bus companies.

A final form of paratransit is the vanpool. Corporate encouragement of vanpooling began in 1973 at the 3M Company in Minneapolis, in response to gasoline shortages. Under corporate vanpooling, the firm buys the van and obtains insurance, leasing it out to an employee-driver who collects fares from other passengers to be turned over to the company. Corporate vanpooling has spread to hundreds of companies, especially in the Los Angeles, Houston, and Dallas areas. An October 1982 census revealed 137 vanpool programs in Texas, utilizing 2,467 vehicles.[33]

Individual vanpooling is another story. The initial pioneers in most states found themselves hauled before state public utility commissions and charged with operating illegal bus lines. In response, California and a number of other states legalized *nonprofit* vanpooling. But organizing a vanpool *for hire* remains illegal in most states without a "certificate of public convenience and necessity" from a state regulatory body—a nearly insuperable barrier for an individual. Yet one of the greatest difficulties in forming a vanpool is finding 8 to 12 other people whose origins and destinations coincide. This problem could be solved easily if small businesses could operate vanpools for hire, advertising their services so that potential riders could find out about them.

3. Transit Brokerage. How can a city or transit agency put into practice the programs and policies discussed in this chapter? How, in other words, can it implement the free market called for by UMTA's paratransit policy? The key to doing so is to rethink the role of the local agency responsible for mass transit. Instead of viewing itself as the principal *provider* of transit, it must come to see itself as a *facilitator* of transit.

This shift in emphasis lies behind what several communities have termed the "transit brokerage" concept. A good example is the pioneering work of the Department of Public Transportation Services (DOPTS) in Knoxville, Tennessee, in the 1970s.[34] Assisted by the University of Tennessee's Transportation Center, the city set up DOPTS in an effort to cut the soaring deficits of the municipal bus service, whose costs were rising while ridership declined. The basic concept was to set up an agency to act as a transit broker, matching up riders with suppliers.

The initial step was to take an inventory of potential transit suppliers, which turned up 27,671 potential seats (including church and school buses, charter buses, and so forth,)—only 3,600 of which were on city buses. The next step was to attempt to expand total ridership, so that ridership gains on paratransit would not come solely at the expense of city bus ridership. To do this, DOPTS identified various barriers to the introduction of van pools and subscription bus service and helped to get them removed. The legislature agreed to exempt private car pools and van pools from common-carrier licensing and regulation. Insurance companies agreed to a simplified form of insurance for van pool operators. Local lenders were persuaded to treat van-pool loans as business loans, rather than personal loans, to permit 100 percent financing. And the city legalized ride-sharing in taxis.

The results were dramatic. In its first two years, DOPTS stimulated the creation of car pools carrying 1,000 people and van pools carrying another 600. Subscription bus service was begun by both private firms and the city bus line—and attracted 1,200 riders. Altogether, in just two years, about 2,000 private cars were removed from the roads during rush hour, as people switched to other forms of transportation.

We've already encountered another agency which sees its role in the same light—the Tidewater Transit District (TTDC) Commission in Norfolk, Virginia. Although responsible for all public transportation in the area, TTDC fulfills this responsibility largely by facilitating the provision of transit, rather than supplying it directly. Whether buying vans and buses and leasing them to private operators, or contracting with taxi firms or other paratransit operators to provide specified services with the firms' own vehicles, TTDC continually seeks out the most cost-effective ways to provide service. Service Development Manager Jeff Becker summarizes the agency's approach as follows:

We are continually trying to expand our line of services in order to provide as wide a range of alternative services to meet the public transportation needs of Tidewater citizens. By working with the private sector, we hope to stimulate additional services at low or no cost to the public. TTDC believes that a wide range of competitive and complementary, privately and publicly provided transportation services will ensure adequate and economical transportation for its constituents.[35]

Several other public agencies are also serving, to some degree, as transit brokers. In Los Angeles, an independent nonprofit organization called Commuter Computer has been promoting and facilitating car pooling and van pooling since the mid-1970s. It also helped the Los Angeles taxi industry introduce shared-ride service, by exploiting a loophole in the taxi regulations. In San Diego, while deregulating taxis, the city also created a staff position called "Paratransit Coordinator." This person's job is to promote the development of a paratransit industry in San Diego by identifying and working to remove regulatory barriers, publicizing new services, and administering demonstration grants from UMTA.

In short, there is far more to public transit than a heavily subsidized, monopolistic municipal bus system. People's transit needs are diverse. In a decentralized, suburban environment, few of those needs can be met well by conventional fixed-rate bus or rail services. Moreover, the costs of a monopoly system—especially one with access to taxpayer subsidies—are certain to be excessive. But the evidence is quite clear that diverse private operators can identify and supply the transit needs of today's metropolitan areas, frequently without subsidy. It's the task of enlightened transit management to see to it that those private operators are given a chance to do so.

Notes

[1]Rochelle L. Stanfield, "Mass Transit Lobby Wins a Big One, But Its Battles Are Not Over Yet," *National Journal*, January 29, 1983.

[2]Charles A. Lave, "Dealing with the Transit Deficit," *Journal of Contemporary Studies*, Spring 1981.

[3]*Transit Fact Book*, American Public Transit Association, Washington, D.C., 1981.

[4]Robert Cervero and Gary Black, "Probable Effects of Eliminating Federal Transit Operating Subsidies," Transportation Research Board, 62nd Annual Meeting, January 17, 1983.

[5]*Trends in Bus Transit Financial and Operating Characteristics 1960-75*, U.S. Department of Transportation, Washington, D.C., 1977, pp. 6-7.

[6]See, for example:R. L. Oram, "Peak-Period Supplements: The Contemporary Economics of Urban Bus Transport in the U.K. and the U.S.A.," *Progress in Planning*, Vol. 12, Part 2, Pergamon Press, 1979. R. Travers Morgan, et al., *Buses in Bradford: Final Report*, England: West Yorkshire Transport Executive, 1975. *Bus Route Costing for Planning Purposes*, Arthur Andersen & Co., England: U.K. Department of Environment, Transport and Road Research Laboratory, 1974.

[7]See Charles Lave, op. cit.

[8]Jack C. Page, "Speed Is the Name of the Game," *Technology Review*, August/September 1980, p.43.

[9]Gabriel Roth and George G. Wynne, *Learning from Abroad: Free Enterprise Urban Transportation*, Council for International Urban Liaison, Washington, D.C., 1982, pp. 40-41.

[10]James B. Ramsey, "Selling the Subways in New York: Wild-Eyed Radicalism or the Only Feasible Solution?" C. V. Starr Center for Applied Economics, New York University, November 1981.

[11]Patrick Cox, "Ringleader of the Rider Revolt," *Reason*, April 1982, p. 48.

[12]*Commuter and Express Bus Service in the SCAG Region: A Policy Analysis of Public and Private Operations*, Southern California Association of Governments, February 1982.

[13]Roth and Wynne, op. cit.

[14]A. A. Walters, "Costs and Scale of Bus Services," World Bank Staff Working Paper No. 325, Washington, D.C., 1979.

[15]See Roth and Wynne, op. cit., pp. 26-27.

[16]Roger F. Teal, Genevieve Giuliano, and Mary E. Brenner, "Transit Agency Use of Private Sector Strategies for Commuter Transportation," Institute of Transporation Studies and School of Engineering, University of California, Irvine, January 1983. (Report No. UCI-ITS-WP-83-1)

[17]A. Jeff Becker and James C. Echols, "Paratransit at a Transit Agency: The Experience in Norfolk, Virginia," Tidewater Transportation District Commission, January 1983.

[18]"Predemonstration Activities of the Westport Integrated Transit System," CACI, Inc., National Technical Information Service, July 1977.

[19]Roth and Wynne, op. cit., p. 47.

[20]G. K. Miller, *Taxicab Feeder Service for Bus Transit,* The Urban Institute, Washington, D.C., August 1976.

[21]"Paratransit: The Coming of Age of a Transportation Concept," in *Paratransit Transportation,* Transportation Research Board Special Report 164, Washington, D.C., 1976.

[22]R. P. Aex, "Demand-responsive Transit and the Integration of D/R Systems with Traditional Transit," *Transportation,* Vol. 4, No. 4, December 1975.

[23]James L. Mercer, "Growth Opportunities in Public Services Contracting," *Harvard Business Review,* March-April 1983, p. 178.

[24]Simon Rottenberg, "An Economic Analysis of the Labor Protection Provisions of the Urban Mass Transportation Act," University of Massachusetts, Amherst, Mass., 1982 (unpublished).

[25]Becker and Echols, op. cit.

[26]Sandi Rosenbloom, "Taxis and Jitneys: The Case for Deregulation," *Reason,* February 1972.

[27]*Effects of Taxi Regulatory Revision in San Diego, California,* and *Effects of Taxi Regulatory Revision in Seattle, Washington,* Urban Mass Transportation Administration, May 1983.

[28]Kenneth W. Heathington, et al., *An Analysis of Two Privately Owned Shared-Ride Taxi Systems,* Urban Mass Transportation Administration, 1975.

[29]Ross D. Eckert and George W. Hilton, "The Jitneys," *Journal of Law and Economics,* Vol. XV, No. 2, October 1972.

[30]These and other examples of jitney service are discussed in Ronald F. Kirby, et al., *Paratransit: Neglected Options for Urban Mobility,* The Urban Institute, 1974.

[31]*A Directory of Regularly Scheduled, Fixed-Route, Local Public Transportation Service in Urbanized Areas Over 50,000 Population,* Urban Mass Transportation Administration, 1981.

[32]Roth and Wynne, op. cit., p. 53.

[33]*The Texas Vanpool Census,* Texas Energy and Natural Resources Advisory Council, Austin, October 1982.

[34]"Transit in Smaller Cities: Ride-Sharing Brokerage," *Municipal Innovations,* No. 20, International City Management Association, July 1977.

[35]Roth and Wynne, op. cit., p. 47.

III

PUBLIC HOUSING

A TALE OF TWO METHODS SIDE BY SIDE

by James P. Butler
President, Housing Opportunities, Inc.

***If** the examples documented here are typical, privatization of public housing might house three families while government houses one. In addition, the private system furnishes superior social benefits.*

In this revealing chapter, the author juxtaposes two low-income public housing programs in one neighborhood in McKeesport, Pennsylvania.

One is a federally administered Housing and Urban Development (HUD) scattered-site program. The other is the privately operated Earned House Ownership Program (EHOP).

Both deliver a quality house. But from then on, the results diverge.

These two contrasting management styles highlight the following eye-opening, bottom-line contrast. The government-administered program acquired its houses for an average cost of $62,854; at the end of five years a remodeled house represented a cost of $153,949, bringing in $125 of monthly rent. The privately operated program acquired houses for an average of $34,200. At the end of five years, a remodeled house represented costs of $57,715, bringing in $285 a month in rent.

Besides the initial higher cost, what are the major costs boosting the cost of the federal house to $153,949? Administration and management costs of $55,000, plus $31,595 in HUD administrative costs, making $86,595 for administration on one house.

This flight from reality is compounded by federal rules which require that craftsmen building houses for the poor be paid significantly more than when they build houses for the rich.

James Butler, wiry and intense, lived with these two projects closely. They were not an academic study to him. This is his lifetime home. He began serving McKeesport and Allegheny County as a social worker, deeply involved with families and their needs. While he did a lot of good for the people in this work, he began to feel that the real root problem was housing. And that he could make a greater contribution by breaking away from other social work to concentrate on neighborhood and housing problems. He felt need of an organization for this work. In 1975, Housing Opportunities, Inc. (HOI) opened operations. James Butler threw all his energies into the work.

Butler's side-by-side comparison gives you very convincing material to use with your colleagues or opponents in leading the drive for privatization of public housing in your community.

While this excellent example confines itself to one city, it can be broadened as a persuasive tool by coupling it with the companion volume, *MORE*.

—The Editors

McKeesport, U.S.A.

The City of McKeesport is located 14 miles up the Monongahela River from Pittsburgh's Golden Triangle. This old steel mill town sits at the center of the Youghiogheny and Monongahela River valley. Like most of its sister communities, which made America an industrial leader in the 30s and 40s, this aging town has fallen on hard times.

In the last 40 years, McKeesport has lost approximately one-half of its population. Many of those who remain are the poor and elderly. McKeesport's illnesses are similar to America's other industrial cities, cities that just a few decades ago were thriving. Now the same communities are dubbed "the rust bowls" of our nation. McKeesport's decline can be measured in a number of areas, including severe drop in the tax base, reduction in jobs, commercial district deterioration and, of course, its neighborhood and residential decline.

The changes in McKeesport's neighborhoods follow classic patterns of urban decline. A major exodus of middle-class residents to McKeesport's suburbs increased the number of vacant and deteriorating houses in the city itself. The percentage of owner-occupied units declined, the percentage of rental units increased, and a housing inventory that consisted of single-family structures was being converted to low-income multifamily units. All of these factors created a serious decline in property values that exacerbated the declining process.

Two Organizations

Two programs are currently operating in the seventh ward, McKeesport's largest residential ward—Housing Opportunities' Earned Home Ownership Program (EHOP) and the McKeesport Housing Authority's Scattered-Site Public Housing Program. Both of these programs are taking vacant, severely deteriorated, single-family units and substantially renovating them for family living.

McKeesport Housing Authority began in 1941 and has grown to three major developments: Crawford Village, a 715-unit project; Harrison Village, 300 units; and McKeesport Towers, a high-rise for the elderly with 200 units. The total population housed in these three areas is 2,264 persons, of which 845 are children under the ages of 18; 863 adults aged 18 to 61; and 556 seniors over 62. The Housing Authority also has 80 scattered-site, Section 8 (minority housing) units and 5 completed scattered-site public housing units. Five more have been acquired and construction is under way.

The staff of the Housing Authority totals 37 full-time employees. Management, legal, and office staff equals 15 persons. Construction and maintenance staffs total 22 persons. Approximately $150,000 of the Housing Authority's $1.6-million administrative budget is for expenses in planning, developing, and managing its 10 scattered-site public housing units.

McKeesport Housing Authority, on the one hand, is locally administered by a board of directors with four volunteers from McKeesport and a full-time executive director supervising the total operation. Housing Opportunities, on the other hand, is a private nonprofit corporation which began in September of 1975 in the dining room of the executive director's McKeesport home. The corporation is governed by 15 volunteer directors from Allegheny County. The volunteer board is made up of builders, bankers, corporate executives, consumers, legal, and accounting professionals.

Housing Opportunities has the multiple mission of helping people to acquire or maintain home ownership and revitalizing older, declining neighborhoods. To accomplish these missions, Housing Opportunities has developed five product lines under these three departments—(1) counseling; (2) research and consulting; and (3) home remodeling and construction.

The counseling department's *Earned Home Ownership Program (EHOP)* provides assistance to first-time home buyers who are not eligible for conventional mortgage financing. An explanation of this program is given in greater detail later in this chapter.

The Delinquent Mortgage Counseling Program, entitled Home Ownership Protective Effort (HOPE), had such a remarkable level of success that banks, savings and loans, and utility companies are hiring our counseling staff to service their delinquent accounts. The HOPE program is an excellent example of *placing social services in the market place*—a concept that is a strong commitment at Housing Opportunities.

Information and referral are other services offered by the counseling department. Last year, Housing Opportunities serviced 556 inquiries on various kinds of shelter issues and was able to direct these inquiries to appropriate resources.

Research and consulting is our newest service line which began in January of 1982. Building on our staff and volunteer experience, Housing Opportunities is selling its expertise in developing the Earned Home Ownership Program (EHOP) and Home Ownership Protective Effort (HOPE) to other nonprofit organizations throughout the country. In addition, our staff also studies housing issues, for example, a two-year study for the Claude Worthington Benedum Foundation on reverse annuity mortgages for senior citizens.

Our final product line is a *Home Remodeling and Construction Company*. Housing Opportunities has performed general contracting work since its incorporation in 1975. As skills in this area grew, and the need to expand the funding base increased, we developed a wholly-owned profit-making subsidiary called Quality Craft, which performs residential construction work. Quality Craft was made possible by a grant from the R. K. Mellon Foundation. This grant was made to study the concept of "feeder organizations" and also provided the seed money to capitalize our wholly owned subsidiary. Quality Craft's profits feed its nonprofit parent. This grant was made in 1979, and the results of our research were reported to the R. K. Mellon Foundation. At the conclusion of our report, Quality Crafts, Inc. was incorporated in March 1981.

Housing Opportunities provides these services in different geographical areas. We concentrate our neighborhood revitalization efforts in two target neighborhoods. Our Delinquent Mortgage Counseling program operates in five counties in southwestern Pennsylvania. Our consulting activities are provided in 12 cities. All of these activities are performed by a full-time staff of 12, plus 6 part-time employees, and 25 active volunteers. Housing Opportunities' total operating budget for the fiscal year of 1983-84 was $430,000.

In Housing Opportunities' first year of operation, 98 percent of its revenue came from contributions and 2 percent came from sales of its services. In 1983, 60 percent of Housing Opportunities' business came from its services, and 40 percent came from contributions. Placing social services in the marketplace and using entrepreneurial activities to fund the delivery of social services is a concept that Housing

Opportunities believed in from its inception. As the years progressed, we at Housing Opportunities became ever more committed to, and ever more convinced that, this approach is a cost-effective way of delivering much-needed social programs.

Now that our community and the two organizations whose programs we will analyze and compare have been given a thumbnail sketch, I will examine the Housing Authority's Scattered-Site Public Housing Program and compare it to Housing Opportunities' Earned Home Ownership Program. The analysis will focus on the key areas of quality of shelter, impact on community, impact on recipient family, and cost effectiveness to taxpayers and community.

McKeesport Scattered-Site
Public Housing

There are, indeed, substantial benefits to the McKeesport Housing Authority's Scattered-Site Public Housing program. The most beneficial feature of this program is the fact that it moves traditional public housing away from the project concepts typical in public housing developments. Public housing recipients live in neighborhood settings away from such large project developments in the area as the Crawford and Harrison Village. Neighborhood locations provide tenants with a reason for taking greater pride in their homes and avoids the social stigma that comes from living in "the projects."

Another social benefit of this program is that a heavy concentration of low-income persons can be avoided in any one location if units are scattered throughout the city thus avoiding the kind of dense packing that these projects so often create. The tenants greatly appreciate living in these spacious units and appreciate the opportunity of living in a pleasant environment.

Scattered-site units are framed two-story, single-family, detached units typical of the housing stock of this neighborhood. The Housing Authority purchased the most deteriorated units on the block that were rehabitable. This was another important plus for the program. Renovating houses that represented the most dangerous health and safety hazards on the block into some of the most attractive homes on the block has had a ripple effect on the neighborhood. The first five units, which the housing authority has completed, are excellent in both workmanship and quality of materials. These units are 40 to 60 years old, but now have a renewed life expectancy of another 40 years. This is because the renovations were substantial and all mechanical systems (plumbing, wiring, heating, and roofing) were totally replaced. In most instances, units were gutted and a new house was literally built inside of an old, but structurally sound, shell.

The negative features of this scattered-site program were inherent in the structure of this public housing program. All of the Housing Authority units pay lower than one-fourth of the real estate taxes that otherwise would be collected for the city, school district, and county coffers if these units were privately owned. To an economically depressed community like McKeesport, this was a significant issue. Approximately 6 percent of McKeesport's population occupied public housing. It is typical for public housing units to be located in poor communities. These communities, however, must provide the same services as all other communities. Yet these areas with public housing do not receive the tax support they would if these units were not owned by the Housing Authority.

As with all other governmental programs, there is, here, of course, large administrative expense. The McKeesport Housing Authority's program is no exception. Even a quick glance at Housing and Urban Development (HUD) handbooks (for construction 7415.1 and accounting procedures 7417.7) substantiates the administrative staff time needed to fulfill all of the regulations involved. Keep in mind that these administrative costs provide no social services to help people improve their economic situation. The operating costs of these programs include only the local Housing Authority's administrative costs. I have not included, but should mention, that the HUD area office in Pittsburgh, the HUD regional office in Philadelphia, and the central HUD office in Washington, D.C., are all involved in delivering this Scattered Site Public Housing program to McKeesport's Seventh Ward. None of these administrative costs has been included in my analysis.

Public housing was designed to shelter people hit by hard times; it was never intended to house generations of poor who were unable to develop the economic independence and to move up and out. Upward mobility will only occur when the social supports are as integral a part of the public housing as roof, walls, and floors.

Excessively high construction cost is the final drawback of this government program. In this case, the McKeesport Housing Authority used its own crew, paid hourly (under the Davis-Bacon wage requirements) for services. This proved to be more costly than if the Housing Authority had put the work out to bid for local subconstractors. Tying professional subcontracting companies to specific bid prices usually insures a lower construction cost. However, subcontractors are also required to pay their laborers according to Davis-Bacon wage guidelines. The Davis-Bacon rates also significantly increased the cost of construction. As absurd as it may sound, the Davis-Bacon Act is a federal law that requires craftsman building houses for the poor to be paid significantly more than when they are building houses for middle-income Americans.

The Earned Home Ownership (EHOP) Program of Housing Opportunities, Inc.

Housing Opportunities has operated its Earned Home Ownership Program in McKeesport's seventh ward since 1975. Housing Opportunities believes that the key ingredient to a stable neighborhood is a high percentage of owner-occupied dwellings. Housing Opportunities' target neighborhood in McKeesport's seventh ward used to be 80 percent owner-occupied. Now the percentage is just under 50 percent. This neighborhood suffers from a migration of one-time homeowners, increasing abandonment, and an old housing stock that reflects deferred maintenance.

Like the Housing Authority, Housing Opportunities purchases the worst vacant property on a block that is structurally rehabitable.

All of Housing Opportunities' rehabilitation work is per-

Government vs. Private Housing

Properties	Acquisition & Rehabilitation Costs	Number of Bedrooms	Number of Residents	Yearly Household Income	Rent or Mortgage Payment
McKeesport Housing Authority's Scattered-Site Program					
1. Beech Street	$59,800	4	4	$14,000 to $15,000	$125
2. Jenny Lind Avenue	$72,930	3	7	$14,000 to $15,000	$125
3. Bailey Avenue	$64,935	3	4	$14,000 to $15,000	$125
4. Evans Avenue	$51,674	3	3	$14,000 to $15,000	$125
5. Packer Street	$64,930	4	4	$14,000 to $15,000	$125
Housing Opportunities' Earned Home-Ownership Program					
6. Beaver Street	$18,454	3	6	$14,000 to $20,000	$200
7. Jenny Lind Avenue	$36,327	3	4	$14,000 to $20,000	$352
8. Jenny Lind Avenue	$48,816	4	5	$14,000 to $20,000	$160
9. Beech Street	$26,178	3	5	$14,000 to $20,000	$291
10. Manor Avenue	$41,164	3	5	$14,000 to $20,000	$350

Public and Private Housing—A Cost Comparison

	McKeesport Housing Authority's Scattered-Site Program	Housing Opportunities Earned Home-Ownership Program
Average cost of Acquisition and Rehabilitation	$62,854	$34,188
Number of Bedrooms	3.4	3.2
Average Family Size	4.4	5.0
Average Household Income	$14,500	$17,000
Average Rent or Mortgage Payment	$ 125	$ 285

formed by Quality Craft which utilizes local subcontractors to perform the work. Housing Opportunities' Earned Home Ownership Program is not required to follow the Davis-Bacon Wage rates. The quality of materials and labor, however, are comparable in both the Earned Home Ownership Program and the Scattered Site Public Housing Program. This results in significant cash savings in rehabilitation that can be used for additional housing for low- and moderate-income families. Housing Opportunities does not follow the Davis-Bacon wage guidelines because construction volume is below federal requirements and much of Housing Opportunities' work is performed with private money.

The Difference

The major difference in the two programs centers on the fact that the Earned Home Ownership family *owns* its unit. This ownership has a stabilizing effect on both the family and the neighborhood. The three taxing bodies—city, county, and school district—also benefit from the newly renovated property being put back on the tax rolls.

Average incomes of families in the Earned Home Ownership Program are similar to those of families in the Housing
Authority's Scattered-Site Public Housing Program. Due to
Housing Opportunities' unique mortgage financing, and individualized counseling, these families have the opportunity
to own their own homes and personally reap the benefits of
home ownership. Adjusting the interest, amount, and terms
of the second mortgage, Housing Opportunities can set
monthly mortgage payments to meet individual circum-
stances. This is another way of stretching subsidy dollars to
provide just enough assistance to make the shelter affordable
to marginal buyers. Increasing the amount of second mortgage monies and reducing the interest rate of first mortgage
loans allow the Earned Home Ownership Program to service
a lower income family.

The counseling which Housing Opportunities provides lies
in the areas of finance, budgeting, insurance, property maintenance, and careers. This counseling is done privately with
each family and lasts anywhere from 6 to 18 months.

Because of the depressed property values in this neighborhood, Housing Opportunities provides a unique second
mortgage which covers the difference between the sale price
and 80 percent of the appraised value. The sale price is
determined by adding the acquisition costs, holding costs,
closing costs, and rehabilitation costs.

An example of how this works follows:

The selling price for a typical unit in this neighborhood is
$40,000. The local bank appraises the property at $34,000,
and the local lender provides the first mortgage for $27,200
at conventional rates.

Housing Opportunities provides a second mortgage for
$12,800 at zero interest deferred. The home buyer makes
payments only on the first mortgage. The Housing Opportunities' loan is paid back when the property is sold. If the
property is sold for less than the $40,000 sales price, Housing
Opportunities suffers the loss, not the home owner. This
program is used as an enticement to get families to reinvest in
our neighborhood without the fear of losing money on a
marginal neighborhood.

Innovative Financing for Home Mortgages

Home Financing	Monthly Payment*
Local lender provides a first mortgage for $27,000 at 12 percent fixed rate for 25 years	$285.00
Housing Opportunities second mortgage provides -$6,810 (0) interest deferred (down payment loan) -$6,000 (0) interest deferred (equity participation loan)	 –0– –0–

*(For total shelter costs you must include taxes, insurance and utilities.)

Continuing our example, let's assume that a client sells his home five years later for $36,500. The first mortgage principal would have been reduced by approximately $1,000, leaving a balance of $26,200. This is paid for from the proceeds of the sale.

$36,500 – Total Selling Price
- 26,200 – Balance of First Mortgage
  10,300
- 1,000 – Closing Costs
$ 9,300 – Total Proceeds

To insure that the EHOP buyers maintain all of the advantages of home ownership, we guarantee that they will receive 25 percent of the balance after the first mortgage, down payment loan, and closing costs are paid. This additional incentive is included in our unique second mortgage loan. The practice of *sharing* the proceeds insures that the buyer has an equitable interest in his property. This fact will help to encourage property improvements and upward mobility of residents.

$ 9,300 – Total Balance
- 6,800 – Down Payment Loan
$ 2,500 – Remainder of Proceeds

$ 2,500 – Remainder of Proceeds
x   .25 – Homeowner's Share
$ 625 – Goes to EHOP Homeowner
$ 1,875 – Complete Payoff of
           Housing Opportunities'
           Loan with the
           Non-Profit suffering
           the loss of $4,025.

Although at this writing only two families have sold their homes, Housing Opportunities has recaptured the principal on its second mortgage loans in both cases. Rising property values and inflation help to protect Housing Opportunities' revolving pool of second-mortgage money. Other municipalities can also direct their community development block grant monies to community nonprofits who establish second-mortgage pools in the same way as Housing Opportunities did.

Targeting a depressed neighborhood and concentrating on an Earned Home Ownership Program will help move the property values to a level that supports a healthy and active private sector involvement. If the Housing Authority's Scattered-Site Program were to increase dramatically in a target neighborhood, their efforts would depress property values and reduce revenues to the three taxing bodies. The benefits that the Earned Home Ownership Program provide these taxing entities are easily measured. The benefits to the families who would otherwise be excluded from home ownership are certain. The impact on these families is substantial, although much more difficult to measure.

The intent of the Earned Home Ownership Program is to support the family—the nucleus of the community and the nation. In addition, the program supports neighborhood revitalization efforts, expands the tax base, and helps to protect other investments in the neighborhood.

The Earned Home Ownership Program is not the panacea for all public housing problems. It can, however, be a more effective way of housing at least 30 percent of the residents now in traditional public housing. In order to house the other

70 percent whose income is too low to fit into traditional homeownership, Housing Opportunities is now developing a pilot Scattered-Site Cooperative. Many of the concepts such as counseling, placing properties on the tax rolls, and special financing are part of this demonstration pilot. If the pilot is successful, the organization will acquire another vehicle to house the very poor in a more cost-effective way, and in an environment that is more conducive to improving the quality of life.

Comparing these two programs for a five-year analysis of per unit cost reflects the serious need for program reform.

I have used a five-year analysis to tie into our other example for comparative purposes. The federal system costs more than $154,000 to produce one unit of housing for a low-to-moderate income family for five years. This government-sponsored program has no money budgeted for social services. It is clear that properly implemented counseling services would assist clients obtain upward mobility and, therefore, could possibly reduce the costs of needed housing subsidies. Almost three families could be housed using the Earned Home Ownership Program's housing model for every one family housed by the public sector. It is painfully clear that the significant changes must occur in federal housing programs.

If Housing Opportunities' pilot had additional money for larger second mortgage loans, plus a mechanism to reduce the rates on first mortgage loans, it could house low-income persons for one-third the cost currently being spent in public housing. The excessive costs of federal housing programs are staggering. Consider all of the families who could be properly housed if common sense and cost efficiency were allowed to operate in helping to shelter our neighbors. If a current Pennsylvania program, entitled the Neighborhood Assistance Act (NAA), were expanded it could provide the mechanism to allow local lending institutions to reduce the interest rates on first mortgage loans (on an EHOP formula basis). This approach would be cost-effective and would allow greater service for more lower-income families.

Annual Housing Unit—Analysis of Costs

	Year					Five-year Total
	(1)	(2)	(3)	(4)	(5)	
McKeesport Housing Authority's Scattered-Site Program						
Acquisition & Rehabilitation	$62,854	$ -0-	$ -0-	$ -0-	$ -0-	$ 62,854
Administrative & Management	15,000	10,000	10,000	10,000	10,000	55,000
Loss of Local Tax Revenue	900	900	900	900	900	4,500
HUD Administrative Costs	6,319	6,319	6,319	6,319	6,319	31,595
Total	$85,075	$17,219	$17,219	$17,219	$17,219	$153,949
Housing Opportunities Earned Home-Ownership Program						
Acquisition & Rehabilitation	$34,188	$ -0-	$ -0-	$ -0-	$ -0-	$ 34,188
Administrative Expenses	250	250	250	250	250	1,250
Counseling Services	3,000	-0-	-0-	-0-	-0-	3,000
Loss of Local Tax Revenue	-0-	-0-	-0-	-0-	-0-	-0-
Rent Subsidy	12,800	1,620	1,620	1,620	1,620	19,280
Total	$50,238	$ 1,870	$ 1,870	$ 1,870	$ 1,870	$ 57,715

In summary, the following chart will help compare and evaluate these two programs:

Public & Private Housing—A Summary

	Improved Benefits	
	Housing Opportunities (EHOP)	McKeesport Housing Authority (Scattered-Site)
Tax Revenues Collected	X	
Lower Cost, Low-Cost Shelter		X
Social Services Provided	X	
Quality Shelter	X	X
Tax Dollars Stretched	X	
Lowered Construction Cost	X	
Lowered Administrative Overhead	X	
Incentives to the Private Sector	X	
Property Values Increased	X	
Upward Mobility Encouraged	X	
Neighborhood Revitalization	X	X
Blighted Properties Eliminated	X	X

As the chart indicates, the Earned Home Ownership Program is superior in providing shelter at reduced cost and also accomplishes much for the vitality of the community. The *quality of life*, though an intangible, is not easily measured; but, in our opinion, the Earned Home Ownership Program has also been superior in this area.

Owning one's home provides a great deal of pride and promotes a sense of accomplishment that directly affects family stability. Many of Housing Opportunities' Earned

Home Ownership families have lived for many years in public housing. Their stories and the impact EHOP has had on their lives is more dramatic than all the other aspects of this innovative program.

Counseling, coupled with the unique financing, provide greater independence and encourage upward mobility. These important areas are not addressed in the McKeesport Housing Authority's Scattered-Site Public Housing Program, nor are they a part of the traditional public housing throughout the United States.

IV

THE FIRE DEPARTMENT GOES PRIVATE

by Lou Witzeman
Private Sector Fire Association

Fire protection is an excellent starting place for privatization, because the successful examples which can be cited are quite clear-cut. The financial advantage is publicly visible. Additionally, the electorate is somewhat aware that fire protection was originally handled by private fire companies, and the volunteer fireman is still active Americana.

This chapter is immediately useful for any local official seeking breakthrough cost improvement.

Author Lou Witzeman instructs with the detail and authority of the national pioneer that he is. Even after 36 years' experience, his big freckled hands look as if they could still handle the one-truck, one-station, one-man fire department he started in 1948 to serve the north suburbs of Phoenix. Rural/Metro, he called it. Initial funding was by individual subscription, later adding contracts with municipalities.

Under his management, Rural/Metro grew rapidly, adding other emergency services. Today, the company serves 20 percent of Arizona's population and parts of Tennessee, New Mexico, and Texas with 205 vehicles, 45 stations and 1,100 employees. Witzeman, the whip-figured chairman emeritus, now moves through the industry on call, here and abroad, setting standards and instructing.

In this chapter he gives clear examples of good operations, complete with the numbers.

One section of this chapter is all by itself worth the cost of a high-priced consultant. That is the hard-won financial analysis procedure for charting the true cost of fire protection, especially identifying hitherto veiled costs assigned to other departments. This financial chart is at once an excellent feasibility study procedure for your own situation and a demonstration tool for presenting the privatization case to your community.

The chapter presents one very startling example, the world's largest private fire company, successfully serving 165 towns, and expanding in a nation often used as the definition for socialism.

Political leaders and city managers are finding privatization of fire protection gives them aggressive fire protection with relief from constant fire department personnel problems and relief from the capital expenses. Operating savings were in the neighborhood of 50 percent, on a per capita basis or 60 percent on a basis of department personnel, while creating another taxpayer, the private fire company.

The companion volume to this, entitled *MORE*, presses for privatization of most government services as a way to reestablish a fiscally sound United States of America. The privatization of many of the nation's 28,776 fire departments could be a giant step in this direction. Lou Witzeman's chapter shows this to be readily accomplishable.

—The Editors

The High Cost of Waiting for Something to Happen

Shed a tear for the Glory Days of the American fire service—they are dying fast. Those halcyon years of professional heroes madly charging about rescuing every blonde on the block, of glorious custom-made fire trucks with 13 coats of lovingly hand-rubbed red paint, have yielded to an era of professional management and screams from taxpayers about the high cost of the fire service itself. A new and very professional breed of fire chiefs is arriving on the scene. And, strange to relate, competition in the form of an upstart private fire service expanding at a rapid rate is now about to challenge one more bastion of governmental enterprise.

The intangibles in judging a fire department's cost-effectiveness have been a bane of government officials for years. Until relatively recent years few attempts were made to analyze them. The core of government's problem has been the difficulty of determining the cost-effectiveness of a service that is "paid to wait" for disaster and geared to handle the worst-case fire problems of a community. The effect was to produce a service that once spent most of its time waiting for something to happen, and the worst-case "something" was a statistical improbability of a nonetheless expensive nature.

The problems of analysis lie in estimating "what would have happened" if a given fire department of a given configuration had not attacked a blaze in the time frame and in the manner that it did. The analysis becomes negative and after-the-fact. Fire losses on a per-capita or per-dollar-at-risk basis are one measurement but they ignore fire problems in differing communities of the same population or dollar at risk. For instance, there is the apples-and-oranges comparison of an old, industrial, factory-and-warehouse city with a new, residential ring city of equal dollar values and population. This is the type of problem that drove city managers up the wall for so many years. The intangibility of the analysis probably contributed to a failure to really study the fire departments because it seemed so nearly hopeless. And in the glorious pre-Proposition-13 days when there was plenty of money to go around (*note:* most government officials didn't think so then, but they surely do now!), cities could pass lightly by the cost-effectiveness issues of their fire departments while zeroing in on the easier analyses of such things as cost of refuse service and manhole covers.

How did the fire service acquire this enviable avoidance of budget scrutiny? For starters, the fire service has had a number of really good image factors going for it. Historically,

• *Firemen were the government's good guys.* They didn't write parking tickets, they didn't dig up the streets in front of business places during tourist season, they didn't pass tax levies.

• *Firemen were heroes.* They charged around town rescuing everything in sight. In time of disaster, they were the taxpayers' savior. They were the role model for countless youngsters who loved to climb into the front seat of the big, red fire wagon and pat the black-and-white Dalmation on the head. Youngsters grew up, but they never forgot.

• *The fire service acquired a mystique.* It was assumed that fire apparatus was something very complicated which could be built only from scratch and at a large cost (custom-made). It was assumed the management and performance of the fire service was a thing unto itself which was different from and did not relate directly to the management of the rest of the city and was imponderable to that city. It assumed a majesty of inviolate tradition in its traditional red trucks, its traditional Roman helmets, doing things in its traditional way in its traditional paramilitary organization.

Historically, the U.S. fire service was an all-volunteer organization, also highly social in nature. Some of the first fire companies were owned by insurance companies. These companies gave the insured a plaque (fire mark) to hang prominently on his property, after he had signed his name on the dotted line. The plaque identified the insuror and guaranteed that its fire company would respond when fire struck.

The fire service grew steadily through the years. It became a full-paid service in most large communities while a more mature, better trained group of dedicated volunteers generally continued to handle small communities. Equipment gradually improved within the limits imposed by the traditional attitude of users. Custom-made fire trucks (still mostly red but with a beginning show of lime-yellow, a safer color) became the standard of the major departments, and the ideal of practically all.

The apex of this pre-Proposition-13 era was reached as the paramedic service became a creature of the fire service establishment. The fire service reached a new high in public adulation as a result of paramedic service delivery. A popular and long-running television show *(Emergency)* led the public reaction to paramedic service as the tube portrayed heroes doing the virtually impossible to the unknowing on the streets of southern California. The reruns continue at this writing. The glamour and jazz of the fire service was riding a new crest. Then came Proposition 13.

Fire Service as a Business

In the final years of the heyday of America's traditional fire service, a new element made a major impact on the scene— the private fire service, organized as a business and offering government an alternative to operating its own fire department. It first appeared importantly in the Phoenix, Arizona, area where Rural/Metro Corporation began serving suburban residential areas. That was in 1948. The firm now serves approximately 20 percent of Arizona's population and is the nation's largest private fire service.

The private sector provides service primarily through individual subscriptions with property owners and *master contracts* with government entities including cities, counties, fire districts, airports, and military installations. The five major firms providing contracted for fire protection in the United States, along with Falck and Zonen of Denmark, have formed the Private Sector Fire Association (PSFA) headquartered at 2006 Broadway, Boulder, Colorado 80302.

The U.S. member firms are Rural/Metro Corporation; Wackenhut Services, Inc.; American Emergency Services, Inc.; Valley Fire Service and O'Donnell Fire Service.

A preliminary list of U.S. providers recently prepared by the association for its membership includes 17 providers serving 36 locations. An undetermined number also serve overseas areas.

Service areas now exist in Arizona, Georgia, Illinois, Oregon, Montana, Tennessee, New Hampshire, Wisconsin, Missouri, Iowa, Oklahoma, Ohio, Florida and Washington. Structural protection is provided in Arizona in Scottsdale, Youngtown, Sun City, Sun City West, Paradise Valley, Fountain Hills, Oro Valley, Tucson Estates, Tucson Country Club Estates and Green Valley, Arizona; also suburban Knoxville, Oak Ridge, Halls, Powell, East Ridge, Tennessee; Elk

Grove, Illinois; suburban Savannah, Georgia; suburban Bill-ings, Montana; Hall County, Georgia; Kennedy Space Cen-ter, Florida; and suburban Grants Pass, Oregon.

Additionally, airports are provided private fire protection in Manchester, New Hampshire; Green Bay and Madison, Wisconsin; Oklahoma City, Oklahoma; Kansas City, Mis-souri; Sioux City, Iowa; and Medford, Oregon.

The PSFA's preliminary list details service provided to eight fire districts, seven suburban unincorporated areas, eight municipalities, seven airports, and five miscellaneous areas primarily consisting of federal government installations of various types. A real duke's mixture of service types.

World's Largest

The largest fire protection firm in the world, in fact, is a Danish firm listed in the PSFA membership as Falck and Zonen. Its existence in Denmark is a philosophical quandary to the many who consider that nation the heartland of socialistic enterprise. Falck and Zonen provides fire protec-tion, wrecker services, rescue and other related emergency facilities with a cadre of some 6,700 employees. It operates more than 2,300 vehicles from 134 locations in Denmark, serving 165 municipalities. It is now branching out into Germany.

The firm traces its history of operation back to 1906, when Sophus Falck opened a salvage station in Copenhagen. In 1908, Falck purchased the first motorized ambulance in the Scandinavian countries and placed it in operation; in 1922 he opened his first fire station. The history of this private fire-service firm in Denmark is thus 61 years old with a record that extends back 77 years.

Denmark's Falck and Zonen has an amazingly similar philosophy to that of U.S. firms. It competes in the market-place by providing a full spectrum of emergency assistance to the public. Services include air and ground ambulance, wrecking, salvage (as in the case of windstorm damage), hot meal programs and, of course, fire and rescue. The firm builds much of its own apparatus. It also operates a Danish automobile club and has extended this operation, primarily for the benefit of Danish tourists, into Germany.

The firm remains a family-controlled organization and operates under Danish governmental regulation.

Operations in the United States

In the United States, the private-sector fire service basically survives and thrives by applying modern business techniques to a tradition-ridden service. Sheer survival dictated the need to improve and cost effectively recreate the functions expected of fire fighters. In the case of Rural/Metro, this led to the firm's building its own trucks, fire stations, providing a mix of paid and paid-on-call employees. The private sector developed the tools and techniques to do the job as well for less. Without cost-effectiveness, the firm would have long been out of business. Survival proved to be great motivation.

In analyzing its service role to the public, the private fire-fighting sector sees itself as virtually the emergency trouble-shooter for all those it serves. The nature of its mission is that of a 24-hour-a-day fast response agency. At three o'clock in the morning, it is one of the few agencies available to perform on an emergency basis. The firm provides necessary domestic crisis-management that may range from water leaks to the removal of desert pests (in Arizona, that means rattlesnakes and gila monsters, among other things).

In Arizona the private sector also, at various times and in various locations, has performed functions that include:

- Periodic dark-house inspections for those away from home

- Combination security-fire patrol in light-attack trucks

- Delivery of medications to invalids in the early morning hours

- Locksmith service to those locked in/out of their autos, houses, bathrooms

- Assembly of refuse containers for one community

- Repair of water meters

Those who provide private service were at first universally acclaimed by the establishment as the village idiots of fire protection. Tenacity and a valid product, however, gradually brought about an acceptance of the new type of organization.

In a nation of some 28,776 fire departments of all types (according to the National Fire Protection Association), the private fire-fighters are still a statistically small factor, but the impact of the management technologies and innovations has been major and the private sector is now growing at a compound rate of approximately 30 percent per year. At this writing, a dozen additional government entities are considering adding their names to the list of those served by the private sector. The PSFA estimates 1,000,000 persons in the United States are being served by these private organizations.

In its structural firefighting service, the private sector addresses itself primarily to what it considers the real world of firefighting. This is not the world of the *Towering Inferno,* (operating in the old and congested cities). The market is best described in the NFPA's *1983 Fire Almanac:*

- 86.6 percent of the nation's estimated 28,776 public fire departments serve communities of less than 10,000 people.

- 98.0 percent of the public fire departments serve communities of less than 50,000 population.

- Communities of 250,000 or more represent only 0.25 percent of public fire departments, and communities in the 50,000–249,999 bracket represent only 1.79 percent.

The private sector thus looks at the numbers—it is good at this sort of thing—and concludes that the real world of fire protection is small and that medium-sized communities are far different from the image the media presents to the public. It is not the world portrayed by the *Towering Inferno.* It is a world of heroic professionals in the volunteer world rather than professional heroes.

When Is Privatization Most Beneficial?

The private sector considers itself able to make the greatest impact on cost-effectiveness (with equal emphasis on both parts of the magic phrase) of a community's development at several points. The first might be when a community is growing rapidly, changing from the small size typified by paid on-call firefighters to a fully paid staff.

Another ideal time is at the formation of a new community. At this point, the private sector can offer a master plan involving water system, fire service, integration of state-of-the-art construction features, and other items which produce a continuing, cost-effective program for the developing area, creating savings not only to the citizens but to the developer as well.

A common point at which controversy enters the picture is when a private company considers providing service that has been provided by an established, union-dominated fire department. The private sector does not consider itself to be in the business of union-busting and, in fact, highly resents occasions when it is called to study a community and then finds its entry on the scene is dictated basically by the diversionary ambition of administrators to twist a union's tail. When and if it does consider serving such communities, the private sector realistically appraises the attitudes of both labor and management and discusses both sides of the issue with the parties involved. Obviously, the private sector must follow the guidelines of federal regulation but finds the moment at which a union contract is under discussion particularly propitious for bringing both elements of the picture—union and city managment—together under the umbrella of private sector service for the community's good.

Political leaders and city managers of many communities have acquired an interest in the private sector as a provider of needed services for a number of reasons. Contracts with such organizations provide a guaranteed cost over a number of years; they provide a layer of insulation between the personnel problems of a governmental fire department and that government. The private sector provides aggressive, cost-effective management. These firms are responsive to the people's needs, combining ambulance, security, alarm systems with the basic fire suppression and prevention functions. Equally important, costs are kept in line. Furthermore, private firms can shift the burden of heavy capital expense from the public to the private sector, and all the while creating a taxpaying firm.

In analyzing federal government fire-service contracts, the United States has found the private sector can generally provide savings of up to 50 percent. This saving, evident to management at other levels of government, remains the primary reason the private sector has become so appealing. The private sector can provide cost-effective services.

The Key Cost Per Capita Criteria

Completion of the charts presented at the end of this chapter will produce a rule-of-thumb cost figure for any fire department's service. These can be simply converted to per capita figures which can in turn be compared with national averages for departments of equivalent population service.

The U.S. Department of Commerce's Bureau of the Census annually publishes fire department costs, grouping municipalities in population brackets, in its *City Government Finances* publication. These data are also available in the *Municipal Yearbook* of the International City Management Association. Data listed below for 1975-76 is from the *1980 Municipal Yearbook,* and that for 1980-81 is from the Census Bureau. The Census Bureau believes an annual rate of increase of 7.5 percent is acceptable in bringing the 1980-81 figures up to the present.

Per Capita Fire Department Cost Estimates

Population Group	1975-76	1980-81	1983-84
More than 1,000,000	$36.37	$49.00	$60.88
500,000 to 999,999	34.71	44.94	55.82
300,000 to 499,999	37.73	49.51	61.50
200,000 to 299,999	33.39	47.31	58.77
100,000 to 199,999	34.09	46.09	57.25
50,000 to 99,999	28.74	40.03	49.73

Limited figures are available for communities of less than 50,000 population but they are too small to be included in this publication.

For fiscal masochists, the following data detailing 1960 per capita fire protection costs by city size might be of interest. It is obtained from the *1961 Municipal Yearbook*. Note city sizes are not the same as those cited in the chart preceding it.

1960 Per Capita Firefighting Costs

Population Bracket	1960 Per Capita Costs
More than 500,000	$9.99
250,000 to 500,000	8.73
100,000 to 250,000	9.43
50,000 to 100,000	8.63
25,000 to 50,000	7.14
10,000 to 25,000	4.95
All cities over 10,000	8.42

The private sector hangs its hat heavily, although certainly not entirely, on its low per capita costs, when compared to those of the public service. With variation of service levels created by the level of emergency medical response a community desires—private-sector fire fighting firms might include any one or more of ambulance, paramedic, emergency medical technician, heavy trauma services—per capita comparisons are somewhat muddled. Scottsdale, Arizona, a city of 103,000 served by Rural/Metro Corporation, enjoys a per capita cost, including all of the factors listed in the charts in this chapter, of $27.37. That dollar figure represents only 48 percent of the national average for cities of its size. The indicated per capita saving of $29.88 is equivalent to $3,078,000 per year. That money could build a lot of roads or pay for a lot of services for the taxpayers of Scottsdale.

Hall County, Georgia, pays Wackenhut Services, Inc., $1,400,000 per year and budgets another $250,000 for its own fire protection and ambulance service. Combined, the per capita cost for its 60,000 citizens of $27.50 represents 55 percent of the national average of $49.73. And for the citizens of the Hall County area, this saving represents a reduction of some $1,333,800, money they would have spent if they were paying as much as the national average service cost for communities of their size.

An interesting comparison of fire departments in the Elk Grove, Illinois, area was recently prepared for the Elk Grove Fire Protection District by American Emergency Services, Inc., which serves that community of approximately 13,500 persons. A total of seven area fire departments including American Emergency Service were compared. At a per capita cost of $36.57, Elk Grove came out ahead. The data obtained by Elk Grove:

The Elk Grove study introduces a new element: In addition to cost per capita, the cost per person employed was computed. On a per capita basis, Elk Grove comes out lowest. It is 40.3 percent lower than the average of the other departments and 14 percent lower than its closest competitor. Cost-per-employe data was obtained by taking total-cost data for departments and dividing it by the number of full-time personnel. It should be noted that in some cases there were also part-time personnel and their impact was not calculated in this study. In other cases, pension plan calculations had to be added to reported departmental budgets to obtain full costs. Elk Grove's closest competitor this time was Community F, which was 13 percent higher. The dollar average for the six departments other than Elk Grove was $42,704, 47 percent higher than Elk Grove itself.

Another study was recently made of the Pima County (Arizona) volunteer fire districts by Rural/Metro Corp. Rural/Metro serves four (36 percent) of the eleven districts in the county which has tax rates assessed through the county government. A fifth district has contracted with Rural/Metro since compilation of the data; it is District G. The study covers tax years 1981 and 1982 and most data was provided by the Arizona Tax Research Association.

A number of facts relative to cost of service are demonstrated by the above chart. They include:

—In 1981, average Rural/Metro-served districts had tax rates only 41 percent of averages for the entire county, and 30 percent of the averages for non-Rural/Metro service areas.

—In 1982, average Rural/Metro-served districts had tax rates only 36 percent of averages for the entire county and 26 percent of the averages for non-Rural/Metro service areas.

Elk Grove, Illinois—A Case Study

Community:	A	B	C	D	E	F	Elk Grove
Population:	38,700	53,600	20,100	66,100	22,200	23,200	13,500
Full-Time Personnel: Total	50	88	41	84	19	41	17
Budget:	$2,566,016	3,929,955	1,538,505	3,356,915	948,628	1,345,870	493,740
Per Capita Cost:	$ 66.31	73.32	76.54	50.79	42.73	58.01	36.57
Cost per Full-Time Employee:	$ 51,320	44,659	37,525	39,963	49,928	32,826	29,044

Pima County, Arizona, Fire District Taxes per $100 Valuation

	Served by Rural/Metro Tax Rate		Not Served by Rural/Metro Tax Rate	
	1981	*1982*	*1981*	*1982*
A	$1.40	$.84		
B	.14	.33		
C			$2.14	$1.55
D	.38	.38		
E			2.60	1.98
F			1.35	1.41
G			1.68	1.58
H			2.60	2.60
I			2.60	2.58
J			1.87	2.60
K	.65	.58		

Throughout the county there was a drop of nine cents per $100 of valuation in the average fire district tax rate between 1981 and 1982 or six percent. Areas not served by Rural/Metro dropped four percent while departments served by Rural/Metro decreased more than four times as much—seventeen percent.

It is numbers such as those cited in Pima County, Hall County, and Elk Grove that arouse government interest in private-sector fire-service.

Cost Accounting in the Fire Business

This chapter discusses in major part the fine art of cost-analysis of the fire service. That fact does not represent confusion between cost and cost-effectiveness. It simply means that fire service financial analysis is a major task of this book. The true cost of fire protection, of course, is a combination of factors including:

• Fire suppression and prevention delivery costs

• Fire losses themselves in current-dollar figures

- Fire insurance costs to the property owners of a community

- Life loss and injury impact

Two financial (self-analysis) charts for fire services are offered the reader. The second chart is simply a short-form recapitulation of the first. The charts are a strange combination of line-item budgets, program budgets, and what have you, but nonetheless carefully prepared to encourage delving into what are usually the problem areas of municipal accounting as it relates to the fire service. The format of the charts is such that where they are presented at first, they are without comments on the various cost factors to be calculated and entered on that chart. The second chart is keyed to the first in such a way that data placed on the first—which in effect becomes a work sheet—can be transferred to the second by line and paragraph number, or letter, to provide a shorter, easier to analyze summary.

The charts are not cast in concrete. If Health and Life Insurance (Benefits Section A.5.) cannot be separated from Other Health Plans (same Section, A.6.), they can be combined on either A.5. or A.6., but the fact should be noted for reference on the first (work sheet) chart for reference. This brings up the question of why the charts were separated in the first place. The answer lies in this: The formatting of the charts and their combination of budget types are aimed at providing the analyst with a tool to, among other things, make fineline distinctions between the routine requirements of prudent management and what sometimes become frills of add-on goodies occurring over a period of time. For example, it would be extremely poor policy to even consider operating without a good basic health insurance policy. Typically, most government and private employers add this type of insurance as the first major non-pay rate benefit. During years of growth, the steady give-and-take of labor negotiation has added to the benefits package.

Health-related benefits have even gotten to the point that eye-glass policies can be purchased as an add-on. Unfortunately, human nature being what it is, we tend to attempt to buy the love and loyalty of our employes with these increases in the benefits package and, again human nature being what it is, once the items get on the budget they tend to stay there forever. And so, a dollar at a time, the "goodies" part of the otherwise basic benefits plan become a major cost factor and a cost that cannot be cut without unfavorable reaction on the part of the employees.

Perhaps somewhat more to the point in this day and age of privatization is the possibility in this particular example that an astute private contractor could bid a lower-cost benefits package consisting of a better health policy, no frills, and achieve a lower net per-employe cost. It has happened. Contracting-out, of course, provides one way for a community to start over from a new zero base and get out from under the fiscal impediments of so many years of dollar-at-a-time add-ons that finally accumulated into a major burden to taxpayers.

Another primary objective of this analysis offered (on the work sheets and chart) is to dig out the bodies frequently buried in municipal accounting methods: the costs of the unfunded pension liability; the overhead implied in other city divisions performing accounting, maintenance, fire inspection for the fire department; the true cost of equipment as reflected by standard depreciation methods instead of the one-shot approach of plugging the entire cost of a pumper, for instance, into the year in which it is budgeted; the cost of water supplies for fire fighting, which are not only direct hydrant costs but include the cost of constructing the basic fire-flow capability of the water mains oversized to provide this flow.

And, finally, the charts are presented in a format to encourage analysis of the impact of modern technology: for instance, part-time payroll is separated from full-time payroll because a $50,000 part-time payroll, as an example, may deliver more trained men to a fire than a $150,000 full-time payroll. The attempt made in the charts is to provide a format with which the innovative, creative administrator can build a better fire service. Good luck!

CHART 1—FIRE DEPARTMENT COST ANALYSIS

	Column 1	Column 2	Column 3

1. Payroll

A. *Uniformed Personnel, Career Staff* $ ____
Comment: This payroll item includes all full-time personnel engaged in suppression, prevention, maintenance, alarm or any other function in which the staff is paid with the same benefits and hired with the same qualifications and procedures as uniformed firefighters. Enter payroll only on this line. Payroll benefits such as pension, etc., are separately calculated. Payroll should include base pay, overtime, any budgeted special payroll allowances such as for educational activity, (but not the tuition and books corollary to such a program), vacations, and sick leave.

B. *Part-Time Staff, Firefighting*   ____
Comment: This payroll item includes the pay of firefighters who are not full-time or career employees. Such personnel would most typically be volunteers, reserves or other paid on-call individuals. They are paid for training and response time but seldom for standby time.

C. *Non-Uniformed Personnel*   ____
Comment: Duties of this staff most commonly include the alarm room, mechanical, inspection, office, and clerical functions—

although not limited to them and certainly not always including them. These employees are usually characterized by an employment procedure less rigid in physical requirement than that of the uniformed personnel or part-time firefighters, less rewarding in benefits, and at time of employment, more detailed in examination of the special skills for which the personnel is hired.

D. *Other Payroll* (insert and describe)   ____

2. Payroll-Related Benefits

Comment: WARNING! The calculation of payroll-related benefits can be most wondrous to behold. A major problem, for instance, is frequently the cost of non-funded pension benefits. A number of items listed below may or may not be applicable to the department analyzing costs on this form—F.I.C.A. (Social Security) costs, for instance, are more typical of private sector payroll benefits than government sector benefits, but do exist in both. Where not applicable, of course, these items can be ignored and the cost entry zeroed out. Since benefits are frequently different for the different classifications of employes listed in Item 1 (Payroll), each payroll category is separately listed for purposes of the calculations below. Obviously por-

$____

tions of payroll deducted from gross pay calculations in Item 1 should not be included in the calculations below.

A. *Uniformed Personnel, Career Staff*

    A.1.   Pension   (current-budget $_____
         cost)

A.2.   Pension (current value of $_____
    unfunded liability)
    Comment: This may be the most difficult calculation involved in this form. If, of course, the pension plan of the department is fully and properly funded, the blank is inapplicable and need not be filled in. If the pension plan is not funded, the blank should be filled in only with the advice of the actuary who regularly analyzes the fund's condition. The item of unfunded liability inserted at this point should be only that portion attributable to the current year's operation.

A.3.   F.I.C.A. (Social Security)   _____

A.4.   Unemployment Taxes   _____

A.5.   Health and Life Insurance   _____

A.6.   Other   Health   Plans—   _____
    dental, optical, major medical, and so forth

A.7.   Industrial Accident (on-   _____
    the-job-injury) costs

A.8.   Other   _____
    Total, Uniformed Personnel $_____

B. *Part-Time Staff, Firefighting*

    B.1. Pension   (current-budget $ ____
           cost)

    B.2. Pension (current value of
           unfunded liability)   ____

    B.3. F.I.C.A. (Social Security)   ____

    B.4. Unemployment Taxes   ____

    B.5. Health and Life Insurance   ____

    B.6. Other   Health   Plans—   ____
           dental, optical, major medi-
           cal, and so forth.

    B.7. Industrial Accident (on-
           the-job-injury) costs   ____

    B.8. Other   ____
          Total Part-Time Staff, $ ____
          Firefighting

C. *Non-Uniformed Personnel*

    C.1. Pension   (current-budget $ ____
           cost)

    C.2. Pension (current value of
           unfunded liability)   ____

    C.3. F.I.C.A. (Social Security)   ____

    C.4. Unemployment Taxes   ____

    C.5. Health and Life Insurance   ____

    C.6. Other   Health   Plans—   ____
           dental, optical, major medi-
           cal, and so forth

    C.7. Industrial Accident (on-
           the-job-injury) costs   ____

    C.8. Other   ____
          Total   Non-Uniformed $ ____
          Personnel

D. *Other Payroll*

    D.1. Pension   (current-budget $ ____
           cost)

    D.2. Pension (current value of
           unfunded liability)

    D.3. F.I.C.A. (Social Security)   ____

    D.4. Unemployment Taxes   ____

D.5.   Health and Life Insurance   ____

D.6.   Other   Health   Plans—   ____
       dental, optical, major medi-
       cal, and so forth

D.7.   Industrial   Accident   (on-   ____
       the-job-injury) costs

D.8.   Other   ____
       Total   Non-Uniformed $___
       Personnel
          Total All Personnel $___

3. Operating Expense:

A.   *Utilities:*

    A.1.   Water $___
       Comment: Even if items
       such as water may be "free"
       to a municipal agency be-
       cause, for instance, it owns
       the water system, a value
       equivalent to what a tax-
       payer would pay for the
       same service must be estab-
       lished.

    A.2.   Electricity/Natural Gas   ____

    A.3.   Telephone (other than for   ____
       emergency alarm facilities)

B.   *Alarm Service*   ____
Comment: This item includes telephone and leased lines and, generally, all nonpayroll expense,
which is covered in Section 1, payroll items. If, however, there is no
direct payroll expense because the
alarm room is operated by an out-
of-budget agency such as the po-
lice department, an allowance for
the fair value of that payroll must
be made here. If there is a budgeted amount for such service as a

payback to the other department performing the alarm room service that budgeted sum may, of course, be used.

C. *Vehicle Operation, Maintenance*
    C.1. Fuel and lubricating oil
    C.2. Maintenance, mechanical and other ____
          Comment: Payroll considerations in maintenance should be handled as for Alarm Service, Item B above.

D. *Office expense*—supplies, office equipment maintenance, postage, printing, and so forth ____

E. *Uniforms* ____

F. *Training* ____
    Comment: Apply payroll consideration as previously discussed, under alarm service expense.

G. *Emergency Medical Service* ____
    Comment: Apply payroll consideration as discussed under alarm service expense.

H. *Fire Prevention, Public Education* ____

I. *Dues and Subscriptions* ____

J. *Research and Development* ____
    Comment: You don't have any? You should!

K. *Miscellaneous* ____
    Comment: This item should be as small as possible! Auditors love to prowl through large "miscellaneous" accounts to see what bodies are buried in them.
    Total Operating Expense $____

4. Overhead:

Comment: "Overhead" for purposes of this analysis is the combination of frequently imponderable and hard-to-determine support costs involved in the fact that the fire department exists as a cog in a larger machine, that machine being the total governmental structure. Calculation of overhead in this section is intended to transfer these support costs to the fire department operation. In a municipality the city personnel department, for example, will usually recruit and qualify new hires; payroll checks are written in the accounting department, which also pays most fire department bills and provides budget status reporting; liability insurance for the municipality is in part attributable to its fire department's operations and should be appropriately distributed. Some municipalities assign general overhead figures to each department. The formulas used for making such determinations approach the unending in variety, but a fair amount of logic can establish a reasonable one in most cases. Examples: the personnel department can be cost-distributed to the fire department in proportion to the number of employees it maintains, or hires on average, or some similar workload measure. Hydrant charges might be determined simply by comparing charges with nearby comparable cities or private utility charges. Accounting department charges might be determined by workload measures including such items as checks/claims processed, percentage of computer operations attributable to the fire service, and so forth.

To provide greater analysis or a method of accumulating some of the individual items involved in this overhead charge, the breakdown below, with some comment on how it may be applicable, might be of assistance:

A. *Insurance—liability, fire, theft, etc.* $____

B. *Accounting*   ____

C. *Personnel Services*   ____

D. *Attorney's Office*   ____

E. *Public Information Office*   ____
Comment: Does this office help with fire prevention week publicity, with code "selling"? Such items might make it a factor in overhead costs.

F. *Building Department*   ____
Comment: Frequently the building department, particularly through its plan checking responsibilities, may have a considerable impact on fire department operations.

G. *Field Operations*   ____
Comment: This department of a city's government may be known by a number of names—here it refers to the division/s that per-

form maintenance of municipal buildings, signing, refuse collection, and so forth—any of which under whatever department may affect the cost of operations of a fire department using this form.

H. *Hydrant Rentals*   ____
    Comment: If no equitable monthly hydrant charge is made to the fire department, some estimate of the amortized cost of installation, maintenance, and actual water consumption must be made. Ideally, amortized cost of fireflow built into the overall water system should also be included.

I. *Other*   ____
    Total of Items A-I, Overhead $ ____
        Total All Items $ ____

CHART II—SUMMARIES OF COST ANALYSIS

	Column 1	Column 2	Column 3
1. Payroll			
A. *Uniformed Personnel, Career Staff*		$ ____	
B. *Part-Time Staff, Firefighting*		____	
C. *Non-Uniformed Personnel*		____	
D. *Other Payroll*		____	
Total Payroll Cost			$ ____
2. Payroll-Related Benefits:			
A. *Uniformed Personnel, Career Staff*			
A.1. Pension (current cost)	$ ____		
A.2. Pension (unfunded liability)	____		
A.3. F.I.C.A.	____		

A.4.　Unemployment Taxes ____

A.5.　Health and Life Insurance ____

A.6.　Other Health Plans ____

A.7.　Industrial Accident Insur- ____
ance

A.8.　Other ____

Total Uniformed Personnel ____ $____

B.　*Part-Time Staff, Firefighting*

B.1.　Pension (current cost) $____

B.2.　Pension (unfunded liabili- ____
ty)

B.3.　F.I.C.A. ____

B.4.　Unemployment Taxes ____

B.5.　Health and Life Insurance ____

B.6.　Other Health Plans ____

B.7.　Industrial Accident Insur- ____
ance

B.8.　Other ____

Total Part-Time Staff, Fire- ____ $____
fighting

C.　*Non-Uniformed Personnel*

C.1.　Pension (current cost) $____

C.2.　Pension (unfunded liabili- ____
ty)

C.3.　F.I.C.A. ____

C.4.　Unemployment Taxes ____

C.5.　Health and Life Insurance ____

C.6.　Other Health Plans ____

C.7.　Industrial Accident Insur- ____
ance

C.8.　Other ____

Total Non-Uniformed Personnel ____ $____

D.　*Other Payroll*

D.1.　Pension (current cost) $____

D.2.　Pension (unfunded liabili- ____
ty)

D.3.　F.I.C.A. ____

D.4.　Unemployment Taxes ____

D.5. Health and Life Insurance   ____

D.6. Other Health Plans   ____

D.7. Industrial Accident Insurance   ____

D.8. Other   ____

Total Other Payroll $____

Total All Payroll-Related Benefits $____

3. Operating Expense:

A. *Utilities*

  A.1. Water $____

  A.2. Electricity/Natural Gas   ____

  A.3. Telephone (Other than Alarm Service)   ____

  Total Utilities $____

B. *Alarm Service* $____

C. *Vehicle Operation, Maintenance*

  C.1. Fuel and Lubricating Oil $____

  C.2. Maintenance, Mechanical and Other   ____

  Total Vehicle Operation and Maintenance $____

D. *Office Expense*   ____

E. *Uniforms Expense*   ____

F. *Training Expense*   ____

G. *Emergency Medical Services Expense*   ____

H. *Fire Prevention, Public Education*   ____

I. *Dues and Subscription*   ____

J. *Research and Development*   ____

K. *Miscellaneous Expense*   ____

Total Operating Expense $____

4. Overhead:

A. *Insurance* $____

B. *Accounting*   ____

C. *Personnel Services*   ____

D. *Attorney's Office*   ____

E. *Public Information Office*   ____

F. *Building Department*   ____

G. *"Field Operations"*   ____

H. *Hydrant Rentals*   ____

 I. *Other*   ____

Total All Overhead $ ____
GRAND TOTAL $ ____

V

SOLID WASTE COLLECTION

by Nancy M. Peterson

Follow an American around *for a day, he leaves a trail... three pounds of rubbish. That is 100 million tons per year for all of us, growing at the rate of 2 percent annually. The privatization of waste handling is farther along than most municipal functions and for the official wishing to start privatization, waste collection and disposal are probably the easiest to get started.*

The author shows that, because of its high visibility, waste management is one of our best entering moves toward privatization of local government services. The citizen sees the private waste collection operation right at her front door and can personally witness its efficiency. The carry-over possibilities to other services becomes favorably apparent.

Author Nancy M. Peterson is editorial director of *Waste Age*, the substantial, hundred-page monthly magazine, published by the National Solid Waste Management Association (NSWMA), 1120 Connecticut Avenue, N.W., Washington, D.C. 20036. Executive director of NSWMA at this writing is Eugene J. Wingerter. The association of some 2,000 companies contains several subdivisions (institutes) devoted to various aspects of the task. They include waste equipment, waste technology, chemical waste, and resource recovery.

In addition to the coverage of solid waste collection, this chapter can also be useful to you in dealing with your local media—the size of the waste-management industry is one of the best-kept secrets from the general public, and yet represents one of the most dramatic industries in the nation. For example, the annual management of our solid waste is an $8-billion dollar job. The private sector already handles more than 70 percent of the residential and more than 80 percent of commercial-industrial waste. Some 10,000 waste-handling companies use 65,000 vehicles and employ 120,000 of us, while serving over 120 million people.

Ninety percent of these companies are small, family-owned businesses, typically operating 5 to 10 trucks and grossing less than $1 million. Among these thousands of firms are a handful of giants operating internationally and listed on the New York Stock Exchange.

The large firms have broadened their function to include chemical waste-handling, hazardous waste disposal, resource recovery, research, sophisticated landfills, cleaning and maintenance of many types including street sweeping, public park maintenance, cleaning of public places, washing the statues. (This is in foreign nations.)

—The Editors

Residential refuse collection is at the top of the list of critical services performed for any municipality or county. About 110 million tons of municipal solid waste (MSW) are generated annually in the United States. That amounts to about 2 to 3 pounds per person per day. The total figure is increasing annually at a rate of two percent, roughly comparable to the population growth.

Residential Solid-Waste Generation in the United States

Type of Waste	Millions of Tons Per Year	Pounds per Person Per Day
Garbage (i.e., food wastes)	17.8	0.47
Rubbish (excluding yard waste)	48.0	1.27
Yard waste (grass, clippings, twigs, leaves, etc.)	18.1	0.48
Bulky waste (large appliances, furniture, etc.)	6.4	0.17
Total	90.3	2.39

Source: Data are for 1971 and are derived from F. A. Smith, *Comparative Estimates of Post-Consumer Solid Wastes*, SW-148 (Washington, D.C.: U. S. Environmental Protection Agency, 1975).

In 1975, Columbia University's Graduate School of Business, under a grant from the National Science Foundation, conducted a comprehensive survey of residential refuse collection systems. The survey, statistically valid for the 2,060 communities in the United States with populations greater than 2,500, represents 52 million people, or about 25 percent of the current U.S. population.

The survey showed that refuse collection by private firms is such common practice that more than 66 percent of the cities surveyed relied on it for at least a portion of their residential refuse collection. Substantially more communities rely entirely on private firms (45.3 percent) than on municipal agencies (32.6 percent).

Types of Service Arrangements

Private firms collect refuse under a variety of arrangements. Private collection (in which a private firm deals with the resident directly) is part of the refuse collection scheme in about 38 percent of the cities. Contract collection (when one or more firms contract with the city to provide service to its residents) is the arrangement in about 20 percent of the cities, while franchise collection (in which a company is granted an exclusive right to provide refuse collection services in a specific area) is the norm in about 8 percent of the cities.

The arrangement differs significantly depending on the size of the city.

Larger cities are more likely to have municipal services. Franchise arrangements are more common in the West. Southern cities are more likely to have municipal collection (although this has changed in recent years as Sunbelt cities have climbed onto the probusiness bandwagon). Northern cities in the East and Midwest favor private collection.

Statistics compiled more recently than those contained in the Columbia University study reflect a trend toward contracting out for refuse collection services. According to the *Public Works Magazine*'s annual survey of refuse collection practices, more cities are planning to switch from municipal collection to contract collection (2.9 percent) than vice versa. Only 1.6 percent of the cities surveyed have switched from private to municipal collection.

Collection of Mixed Residential Refuse

Refuse Collector	Number of Cities	Percentage of Cities	Number of Cities With Only One Kind of Collector	Percentage of Cities With Only One Kind of Collector	Percentage of 2,052 Cities
Municipality	768	37.4%	668	41.6%	32.6%
Private Firm	1,368	66.7%*	929	57.8	45.3
Self-Service	376	18.3	10	0.6	0.5
Other	19	0.9	N.A.	N.A.	N.A.
Column Sum	2,531	123.3	1,607	100.0	78.3
Total Number of Cities	2,052	100.0			

Notes: Because many cities have more than one kind of refuse collector, the number of types of collectors is greater than the number of cities.

The total number of cities reported in this table is only 2,052 because 8 of the 2,060 cities have collection systems only for *separated* residential refuse, not for *mixed* residential refuse.

*That is, private firms collect at least some of the mixed residential refuse in 66.7% of the 2,052 cities.

Service Arrangements for the Collection of Mixed Residential Refuse

	Total	Municipal #	Municipal %	Contract #	Contract %	Franchise #	Franchise %	Private #	Private %	Self-Service #	Self-Service %	Other #	Other %
Total	2,531	768	30.3	420	16.6	166	6.5	782	30.9	376	14.9	19	0.8
Population Group	2,531												
≧250,000	37	27	73.0	4	10.8	0	0	4	10.8	1	2.7	1	2.7
50,000–249,999	268	149	55.6	25	9.3	22	8.2	41	15.3	28	10.4	3	1.1
10,000–49,999	706	242	34.3	152	21.5	59	8.4	170	24.1	81	11.5	2	0.3
2,500– 9,999	1,520	350	23.0	239	15.7	85	5.6	567	37.3	266	17.5	13	0.9
Geographic Region	2,531												
Northeast	981	186	19.0	213	21.7	22	2.2	382	38.9	176	17.9	2	0.2
North Central	715	143	20.0	111	15.5	16	2.2	330	46.2	107	15.0	8	1.1
South	469	341	72.7	28	6.0	34	7.2	33	7.0	27	5.8	6	1.3
West	366	98	26.8	69	18.9	93	25.4	37	10.1	66	18.0	3	0.8
Form of Government	1,799*												
Mayor-council	876	374	42.7	214	24.4	42	4.8	178	20.3	64	7.3	4	0.4
Council-manager	724	319	44.1	109	15.1	103	14.2	100	13.8	87	12.0	6	0.8
Other	199	54	27.1	32	16.1	5	2.5	60	30.2	45	22.6	3	1.5

Note: This table shows the distribution of *arrangements*, not the distribution of *cities*. There are a total of 2,531 arrangements in the 2,052 cities.

*Information on form of government was not available for some cities.

The attraction of contract collection is twofold: cost and efficiency. According to the Columbia University study, cities can save up to 30 percent of the cost of refuse collection by switching to private contracting, which operates with certain pronounced differences:

- *Using fewer workers per truck.* The average crew size for municipal residential collection is three to four workers, while the average crew size for a private company's residential route is one to two workers.
- *Using larger capacity refuse trucks.* The typical municipality's refuse collection truck holds 16 to 20 cubic yards, whereas the average private truck holds 25 cubic yards. Larger capacity trucks mean fewer trips to the landfill and less backtracking over already covered routes.
- *Less absenteeism.* The absentee rate for private workers is nearly half that of municipal workers. That means that municipal collection departments are often overstaffed to compensate for the high absenteeism.
- *Using an incentive system* directly related to performance to achieve higher productivity.

The difference in cost between public and private collection may be far greater than the numbers indicate. According to the Columbia University research project, cost-accounting procedures for municipalities understate the real costs by about 30 percent for the following reasons:

- Capital costs of refuse-collection vehicles do not always appear in the budget of the refuse collection department.
- The cost of interest on municipal bonds is rarely ascribed to the refuse collection service.
- The cost of fuel, oil, tires, and other vehicle supplies, as well as construction, maintenance, and operation of garages may be assigned to a centralized vehicles department. Labor costs for vehicle maintenance also may appear under other departments or programs.
- The cost of fringe benefits may appear under a centralized accounting entry.
- The cost of supplementary workers borrowed from other departments to fill in during absences of regular refuse

collection workers is often not charged to the collection activity.

- Overhead costs of city executive and staff agencies are similarly ignored.
- If the municipality is self-insured, the cost of liability claims paid are seldom charged to the service which incurred them.
- The cost of insurance premiums for vehicles and personal liability of the refuse collection department and of fire insurance premiums for departmental property are also often excluded from the department's budget.

A private business must figure all of these expenses into its operating costs. Although any calculation of real costs for municipal refuse collection should include these items, many cities neglect to figure in these costs.

Lower costs, however, are not the only benefit of contracting-out city refuse collection. Contracting out offers city officials an opportunity to introduce labor-saving and productivity gains without assuming direct political liability for unpopular actions. Furthermore, a city can anticipate future costs through the contracting process.

Many municipal managers feel that contracting out presents opportunities for better management and greater flexibility. H. Edward Wesemann, a city manager with extensive contracting experience and author of *Contracting for City Services,* says contracting has these advantages:

- Budget control—Costs under a contract are precisely known in advance.
- Cutback management—Contracted services can be reduced without the necessity of an employee layoff, unemployment compensation costs, and idle equipment.
- Peak periods—Contractors, not the city, must manage personnel to handle peak and slow periods.
- Public popularity—The public has long perceived that the private sector is more productive. The objective citizen views contracting as sound, businesslike management.
- Reduced overhead—Having fewer employees means that personnel, payroll, and supervisory costs are reduced.

Having fewer employees also means that less equipment and equipment maintenance and building space are needed.

- Community involvement—By working with the government, private businesses become more involved in the community and have a greater recognition of their interdependence.
- Productivity measurement—Even if a contract is not entered into, the feasibility study involved provides an important measure of how well a particular municipality is performing in comparison to private industry. It also pinpoints areas where productivity improvements can be made.
- Greater objectivity—Because contracted services are once removed from the municipal organization, budgetary decisions can be made with less departmental politics.
- Fast startup—New programs, services, and projects can be started immediately without hiring and training employees and without delays in purchasing equipment.
- Specialized skills—Contracting provides employees with specialized skills that could not be justified in full-time employees because of limited need for those skills.
- Increased planning—By freeing department directors from the day-to-day worries of operating crews of employees, there is more time for planning.

Experiences in Privatization

While the motivations vary for converting from municipal to private refuse collection, in the final analysis, the result of that change—cost savings—is the big story.

In a study of ten communities that underwent a conversion from public to private refuse collection, Columbia University Graduate School of Business researchers found that contracting out reduced the costs of collection for every municipality. In the first year of the contract alone, costs were reduced by nearly 30 percent in one city and never by less than 7.5 percent. It is notable that this occurred without any deterioration in the levels of service.

Cost Comparison of Residential Refuse Collection Before and After Change

City Name	Year of Change	Number of Households	Annual Municipal Cost in Year Prior to Change (per HH)	Projected Cost of Municipal Service (per HH)	Annual Contract Cost (per HH)	Net Transition Gain (Cost) (per HH)	% Change in Cost (3) − (4)
Berwyn, Ill.	1976	15,800	$41.67[1]	$43.31	$40.06[1]	NA	− 7.5%
Pekin, Ill.	1976	10,334	$76.18	$81.32	$70.21	NA	−13.6%
Covington, Ky.	1975	17,569	$30.28	$30.28	$26.11	$ 7.22	−13.7%
Middletown, Ohio	1972	16,200	$27.34	$29.83	$21.00	$ 4.58	−29.6%
Gainesville, Fla.	1977	14.921	$59.17	$62.79	$48.12	$18.60	−23.4%
Camden, N.J.	1974	25,000[2]	$62.81[1]	$67.67[1]	$54.01[1]	$ 4.73	−20.2%

[1]Cost include disposal

[2]Camden's 25,000 reflects total number of refuse collection customers and includes some commercial stops.

Cost Comparisons in Cities with Mixed Public/Private System

Name	Year Portion of City Contracted Out	Municipal Cost	Contract Cost	% Difference
Akron	1973	$49.55	$37.41	24.5%
Kansas City	1971	$37.72	$19.09	49.3%
Oklahoma City	1976	$57.98	$49.90[1]	13.9%
New Orleans	1977	$47.29[2]	$41.32[2]	12.0%[2]

[1]Average cost for three contract sectors.
[2]Compares before and after costs in the one district that was contracted out.

Although cost savings are the most obvious, cities realize other benefits from contracting out. Private contractors enable municipal governments to rid themselves of the difficult task of supervising sanitation work and the sometimes militant or unproductive workforce. By retaining certain monitoring functions, city managers retain the *responsibility* for efficient refuse collection—a more sophisticated managerial function than actually running the sanitation operation.

Ten Specific Cities Make the Decision

In studying why some cities decided to contract for refuse collection, it is important to remember that refuse collection is a service that brings the public and local governments into regular contact. Hence, the service will come under scrutiny from both groups.

In most of the cities examined in the Columbia University study, when it seemed likely that refuse collection would affect the performance of a local government—or public perception of it—officials began to seek ways to deflect attention and shift responsibility for the problems. Finding a private company to shoulder that responsibility proved to be an effective solution.

The ten cities described in this section all had populations greater than 30,000 and were located in different parts of the United States. Six of the ten were run by city managers while the other four were each governed by elected officials—a mayor and a city council

Characteristics of Ten Case-Study Cities

Region	Form of Government	
	City Manager	Mayor Council
Northeast		Camden, New Jersey (103,000 population)[1]
North Central	Middletown, Ohio (49,000 population)	Berwyn, Illinois (50,000 population)
	Pekin, Illinois (35,000 population)	Akron, Ohio (275,000 population)
	Kansas City, Missouri (507,000 population)	
South	Covington, Kentucky (52,000 population)	New Orleans, Louisiana[2] (593,400 population)
	Gainesville, Florida (65,000 population)	
	Oklahoma City, Oklahoma[2] (375,000 population)	
West		

[1]All populations are 1970 census.
[2]Contracted out a portion of the refuse collection responsibility.

A variety of reasons prompted these city officials to contract with private companies for refuse collection. A major factor stimulating the change from public to private collection was increasingly stringent federal and state regulation of solid waste disposal. Typically, a city was compelled to close down its landfills because it was unable or unwilling to comply with costly environmental regulations. Those cities then started using landfills owned and operated by private companies. It was a short step from using private disposal facilities to using private collection services. These cities also switched to private collection because of financial restrictions, an unmanageable workforce, or a shift of political power.

These cities were attracted to the private sector because contractors could relieve governments of the responsibility of directly managing and maintaining effective refuse collection services.

Major Factors Motivating the Change

Location	Benefits
New Orleans, Louisiana[1]	closing down of municipal incinerators
Pekin, Illinois	closing down of municipal landfill
Oklahoma City, Oklahoma[2]	city sells all its disposal sites
Akron, Ohio	federal funding, stimulating a combined refuse/trash service
Kansas City, Missouri	federal funding, stimulating a combined service
Gainesville, Florida	reduce costs, raise productivity
Camden, New Jersey	circumvent a recalcitrant workforce, upgrade productivity
Covington, Kentucky	reduce costs
Berwyn, Illinois	Republican council's desire to undermine Democratic mayor
Middletown, Ohio	circumvent recalcitrant union

[1]New Orleans is difficult to classify as to a motivating factor. External reasons stimulated a search for refuse collection alternatives. This coincided with shifting political coalitions affecting the strength and status of the sanitation bureaucracy.

[2]In Oklahoma City, again internal and external factors coincided. The city's action in selling its site was directly responsible for introducing the private sector to refuse collection. However, the city also was searching for ways to divest itself of an inefficient workforce and vehicles.

New Orleans, Louisiana

In New Orleans, the U.S. Environmental Protection Agency (EPA) had mandated closing several municipal incinerators and a substandard landfill. City officials decided to let private contractors handle collection services and take the responsibility for locating an acceptable disposal site. This decision was simplified by disenchantment with the city's unresponsive and unproductive workforce. Furthermore, the sanitation division had been a patronage organization over which the new mayor had little control. Thus, private contracting represented an ideal opportunity to increase productivity, reduce costs, and enhance the mayor's political strength.

The private connection, established when the city began using the privately owned landfill, already existed. As part of its campaign for the contract, the company provided cost-and-service analyses as well as information about other cities that had implemented private collection. In doing this, the company became part of the decision-making process, helping to prepare bid specifications, and to determine what would be necessary to maintain the level of service.

Although a power struggle between the head of the sanitation department and the mayor forced a delay until the sanitation workforce had diminished a bit through attrition, the city proceeded to contract out 10 percent of the city's waste.

Implementation was relatively easy because the workers' union also had organized the private hauling firm and even negotiated a contract with the company requiring two-man crews. Interestingly, its contract with the municipality required three-man crews!

Smaller two-man crews were one source of the 12.6 percent cost savings. The contractor also used larger vehicles from which he achieved greater productivity.

Oklahoma City, Oklahoma

Oklahoma City experienced similar difficulties. New federal regulations requiring expensive environmentally related improvements encouraged the city's decision to close its municipally run landfills. Officials pondered the alternative: private landfills. It occurred to them that they could also contract for private collection. If economies of scale worked for others, it could work for them. The prospect was all the more attractive because the city faced large wage demands from its workers. City managers, however, felt that they had a core of efficient workers and well-maintained vehicles. They were reluctant to discard them. As in New Orleans, they resolved this problem by contracting out a part of city collection. In this way, they eliminated the nonproductive elements of the department and consolidated the tasks of the bureaucracy without threatening its existence.

The workers' union was relatively weak in Oklahoma City and made little attempt to block the change. The contractor reduced crew size from three to two and also decreased the number of other operating personnel. These actions reduced city collection costs by 14 percent.

Pekin, Illinois

Pekin underwent a more precipitous change to private collection when its landfill was ordered closed by state authorities. Through a vigorous marketing program, the company operating the area's private landfill persuaded the city to contract for refuse collection as well. The company conducted a cost study of the city's refuse collection system, showed city officials their research and design facilities, and participated in numerous council meetings to argue the case for contracting out.

In Pekin, officials also saw the contract alternative as a way to avoid giving in to wage demands of city workers. Union opposition to the switch received little support and the transition moved forward, though the city let go all of its 23 sanitation workers.

Cost savings were achieved by a reduction in crew size, the use of new vehicles owned by the contractor, and a worker-incentive system that increased productivity. (Workers were paid for a full day and allowed to return home as soon as they had finished their routes.) In the first year of the contract, the city saved 14 percent of its former refuse collection costs.

Kansas City, Missouri

In Kansas City, the situation was different. City officials turned to private contracting after they had expanded service in an effort to avoid expanding the municipal workforce.

The expanded service came about as the city sought to provide a level of service in inner-city neighborhoods equivalent to that available in outlying areas. Kansas City had received federal funds in order to accomplish this.

The contractor spent 49 percent less than the city to provide the same collection service. This huge difference, to a large extent, reflected a difference in fringe benefits paid to private workers.

Akron, Ohio

Akron also had received federal funds to institute a combined wet-and-dry trash collection program in its inner city. These additional funds were used to contract with a private firm for inner-city refuse collection. As in Kansas City, only a portion of the city's collection was contracted out, and neither manpower nor equipment was listed by the public works department. The contractor provided the same level of service as the city sanitation division, but at a cost 25 percent lower. Again, the contractor used smaller crews (three instead of four men) and larger trucks.

**Reasons for Cost Differentials
Between Public and Private Sector**

City	% Savings Between Municipal and Contract Sectors	Reasons for Differential
Akron, Ohio	25%	Smaller crew size (four to three man) Contractor uses larger trucks
Kansas City, Missouri	49	Differing wage and fringe rates
Oklahoma City, Oklahoma	14	Reduced other operating personnel
New Orleans, Louisiana	13	Reduced crew size (three to two man) Reduced total number of vehicles Purchased new vehicles

Camden, New Jersey

As Camden's financial resources began to diminish, a public outcry arose over deteriorating service and high over-

time paid sanitation workers. This was accompanied by the
sanitation department's resistance to all attempts to increase
efficiency and cut costs. Spurred by the prospect of unioniza-
tion of city workers, the mayor raised the alternative of
privatization. The process of change was temporarily stymied
by worker opposition encouraged by the public works super-
intendent. The opposition was strong enough to force the city
to guarantee that no worker would lose his job, but officials
went ahead with the conversion and signed a contract with a
private company to provide refuse collection services.

Ultimately, privatization saved the city 20.2 percent in
refuse collection costs. The contractor was able to do this by
trimming expenses across the board. He reduced the number
of routes, the number of workers, the number of vehicles,
and fringe benefits for workers. Despite these cost-cutting
measures, the level of service remained the same and the
contractor was able to raise wages and purchase newer,
larger, more efficient collection vehicles.

Gainesville, Florida

The decision to seek an alternative to municipal refuse
collection in Gainesville was also sparked by budgetary re-
straints. City officials were concerned about the rapid increase
in the municipal workforce and had already reduced the
collection frequency by half. Nonetheless, costs continued to
rise.

As city officials learned more about private contracting
through national waste conferences and about companies
operating in and around Gainesville, the private alternative
became more attractive. City management viewed contracting out as a way of stabilizing cost increases at certain
levels for a given period of time (the period of the contract).
There was virtually no union opposition to the switch to
private collection even though city sanitation workers were
unionized.

The savings in the first year amounted to 23 percent—a
result of reducing crew size from three to two men and
because new vehicles purchased by the contractor achieved
greater productivity.

Berwyn, Illinois

In Berwyn, labor problems and pressure for pay increases provoked official interest in contracting out. The threat of a third strike in just about as many years, coupled with enormous political conflict between the mayor and city council intensified the council's efforts to contract out refuse collection despite mayoral opposition. Council members viewed contracting as a way of cutting costs and eliminating a source of political patronage for the mayor.

Union resistance, complete with sabotage of collection vehicles, a near-general strike and lengthy court battles, proved costly. As a result, implementation of the contract was delayed. Finally, however, the change occurred. Although the city arranged for its workers to be given hiring priority with the private contractor, after three months only three remained at work with the company. The contractor was able to save the city 8 percent in refuse collection costs by using smaller crews, vehicles with a larger waste capacity, and by consolidating collection costs.

Covington, Kentucky and Middletown, Ohio

Although their reasons for turning to a private refuse contractor were different (Covington officials were eager to reduce costs, while Middletown officials wanted to circumvent the problems caused by a recalcitrant union), both cities experienced strong union opposition to the move.

The union in both areas enjoyed public support and turned to the courts to prevent the cities from contracting out their refuse collection services. In each case, however, the judge ruled against the union, and each city proceeded to sign a contract.

Covington absorbed almost all of its sanitation workers, but the city of Middletown laid off most of its workers. (The labor problems appear to have been more serious in Middletown.)

Both cities enjoyed fairly dramatic cost savings through the contractor's reduction of crew size from three to two men and the purchase of new vehicles. In Middletown, the contractor instituted an incentive system for workers while in Covington the company reduced worker fringe benefits. Covington saved 14 percent in the first year of the contract, and Middletown 30 percent.

Reasons for Cost Savings for Privatization

City	Percent Savings in First Year of Contract	Reasons for Savings
Berwyn, Illinois	8	Reduced crew size (three to two man) Increased vehicle capacity Rationalized routes
Pekin, Illinois	14	Reduced crew size (two to one man) Instituted incentive system* Bought new vehicles
Covington, Kentucky	14	Decreased fringe benefits Reduced total manpower, no reduction in crew size Purchased new vehicles
Middletown, Ohio	30	Reduced crew size (three to two man) Added incentive system Purchased new vehicles
Gainesville, Florida	23	Reduced crew size (three to two man) Purchased new vehicles
Camden, New Jersey	20	Reduced number of routes Reduced total number of drivers and collectors Reduced number of vehicles Purchased new vehicles Substantially reduced fringes, raised wages

*When workers complete route they go home, paid for full day.

The Bottom Line

Clearly privatization saves money. The reasons are also clear: profit-and-loss incentives are powerful. An entrepreneur must organize and operate in such a way that he will profit, yet he must perform, or lose to his competitors. Competition assures that the contractor saves money for the customer. Suppliers who must bid on a contract regularly against competitors who may best them are stimulated to do the best job possible at the lowest feasible cost.

Causes of Resistance

If privatization is better, why don't more cities contract out for refuse collection? The answer is that they do in a growing number. Remember, private firms collect residential refuse in twice as many cities as do municipal agencies. Nevertheless, there is still strong resistance to the concept. That accounts for reluctance of many city governments to turn to the private sector.

One fear is that private firms will cost more in the long run. The evidence concludes otherwise. Numerous and extensive studies comparing government and private services have found that those services cost less when provided by the private sector under competitive conditions.

Another objection often cited in arguing against privatization is that it will lead to corruption, bribery, and kickbacks. For any bribery attempt to succeed, there must be someone willing to accept money. This begs the question, however, which is how to avoid such a situation in the first place. Corruption can be avoided through rational, open-bidding procedures, and objective selection standards—with keen monitoring of the process to ensure that both sides follow the rules. The response to this is to make the process a matter of public record and hold all decision-making sessions in public.

Resistance to privatization is often rooted in the belief that it is anti-labor and will eliminate public-service jobs. Although, in some cases, privatization does reduce the workforce, one way to ease the burden is to require the contractor to give government workers preference in filling job openings created by the contract. In any case, eliminating unnecessary and wasteful practices (such as overstaffing) is in everyone's interest—the taxpayer, the consumer, and the labor union.

The view that public services should not be organized for profit stems from distaste for the idea that people can profit by supplying vital needs of others. This argument, however, seems reserved only for public services. Most people do not consider it immoral for surgeons to profit from life-saving surgery. Profit-making is an organizational principle that serves as a basis for structuring the business of society as effectively and efficiently as possible. It should, above all, apply to public service.

As natural and financial resources continue to diminish, it is important for the public and its government to think clearly about existing service arrangements. Are they efficient? Are they effective? Are they economical? Concerned citizens should consider the possibility that those services are simply businesses that can be operated by private companies and paid for by their customers. A shift to private enterprise is in order.

VI

PRIVATIZATION OF HOSPITALS

by Michael D. Bromberg and Mark J. Brand

Navarro County Hospital in Texas was old, losing money, and about to lose its accreditation. To put it in shape would require $12 million. The county turned it over to a private hospital corporation which is building a new hospital right beside the old one. The old one cost the taxpayers $50,000 a year to operate. The new one is expected to *pay* taxes of $316,000 a year.

That is only one example of the dramatic turn-arounds cited in this brief, intense chapter.

If you are leading a movement for the privatization of a city or county hospital, this chapter can be a powerful tool in persuading your colleagues and opponents. If your opponents are concerned that a private operator will skyrocket prices to patients, the author gives an excellent example for retaining control.

If your opponents are concerned that privatization will eliminate indigent care, the author gives an example for insuring against that.

If opposition is rooted in egotistical desire for control, well . . . that is the race's greatest and most ancient retardant. But the authors supply a workable solution via the use of hospital management firms.

The main theme of the companion volume to this book, *MORE,* may be useful to you in building support for hospital privatization. It demonstrates the compounding advantages from privatization: the flexibility to shop for best value leads to efficiency, which leads to higher use of the service, which leads to profitability, which converts the service from a tax-user to a tax-payer, which leads to citizen tax relief, which enhances the well-being of the community.

Nowhere does that spiral of benefits work more swiftly and effectively than in hospitals.

Authors Michael D. Bromberg and Mark J. Brand of the Federation of American Hospitals (FAH) are in the mainstream of the massive healthcare information flow. Michael Bromberg, referred to by *The Congressional Quarterly,* Jan. 7, 1984 as "the single most effective health lobbyist operating on Capitol Hill," is the executive director of FAH. While the American Medical Association (AMA) is considered the most powerful lobby in medicine, the *Congressional Quarterly* states, "There are many who think the premier individual health-related lobbyist is Michael Bromberg. Bromberg is legendary."

His legendary influence comes from many assets. One of these is the exemplary staff of FAH which includes co-author Mark J. Brand. But Bromberg's most influential asset is an encyclopedic knowledge of the hospital industry. Legislators trust him.

Beyond this article, the Federation of American Hospitals is the source of further information on hospital privatization (1111 19th Street, N.W., Washington, D.C. 20036).

—The Editors

If your community hospital is: (1) an aging institution; (2) understaffed; (3) has poor, outdated, or insufficient equipment; (4) lacks sufficient operating funds; (5) has no reserve funds and limited access to new funds; (6) has a small tax base; and/or (7) exists outside a major metropolitan area, you should consider selling your hospital or having it managed by a private hospital management corporation.

Why a Management Company?

What are the advantages to your community of selling to a hospital chain? In one word—taxes.

Your county or community will no longer be financially burdened by supporting a hospital, and will instead, receive generous compensation from the sale. In addition to the sale price, an investor-owned-for-profit hospital pays into the local tax fund, providing further revenues for the community.

A management company has the wherewithal to make needed improvements because of its access to equity markets. "These corporations have access to capital through sale of stock. Because of that," states Michael D. Bromberg, executive director of the Federation of American Hospitals, the trade association of investor-owned-for-profit hospitals and hospital management companies, "more capital is being made available through new sources of equity financing. The results have been improved quality of care and the introduction of needed technology in areas of the country that otherwise would not have had access to modern medicine. Additionally, private investment also frees up government funds for other infrastructure repair that is so critically needed.

"For example, the multi-billion-dollar Hospital Corporation of America (HCA)—which owns 212 hospitals in the United States and manages 150 more for other owners—raised $210 million last year by selling three million shares of stock."

The quality of hospital care generally increases because of improvements in the management of funds, services, and personnel. A strong financial and organizational atmosphere attracts—and keeps—better medical and administrative personnel.

A management company is able to purchase technologically advanced equipment at lower prices because it has purchasing contracts with vendors who provide corporate discounts for bulk buying.

Through efficient management, personnel assignments, and increased quality of care, length of patient stay can often be decreased, thereby reducing costs for the hospital, the patient, and third-party payers.

Corporate access to, and use of, sophisticated central data-processing banks creates more efficient administrative and billing procedures at a lower cost.

Hospital management companies have played a leadership role with regard to cost containment. Some of the steps that these corporations have undertaken to achieve this are:

- Management systems development and implementation of services in the form of industrial engineering support are in place.
- Centralized physician recruitment programs have been instituted.
- Third-party reimbursement expertise to fill out cost reports and appeals is made available to all hospitals, reducing the need for expensive consulting services.
- Standardization with regard to buildings and equipping hospitals.
- Lower insurance costs often made possible through creation of insurance companies.
- Where possible, supplies within hospitals have been standardized reducing inventory and improving prices.
- Providing administrators with resource documents detailing organizational and procedural methods to contain costs.

With such increased financial capability, your hospital will be able to offer increased medical services to your community.

How Big Is the Trend Toward Investor-Owned and -Managed Hospitals?

At least five major chains—American Medical International, Hospital Corporation of America, Lifemark Corporation, National Medical Enterprises, and Humana—have billion-dollar-plus revenues annually, and all are continuing to grow. Of the 7,000 or so hospitals in the United States, slightly more than 1,100 are now investor-owned. Nearly 300 more hospitals are managed by profit-making companies. Since 1975, at least two dozen government-owned hospitals have been acquired by for-profit chains and subsequently made great strides in improving the quality of care they provide.

A classic example of one such success story took place in 1980 when York County, South Carolina, sold its General Hospital in Rock Hill to American Medical International (AMI). Not only did the county get out of the tax-draining business of running a hospital but received $3.4 million from the sale, with an additional $5.4 million from leasing arrangements with AMI. AMI also built a new $28-million medical center in the community to replace the aging county hospital. Moreover, the quality of care at the AMI-run facility improved markedly. For example, the company expanded the medical staff with 13 badly needed doctors and three specialists. Another indication of AMI's superior performance is that occupancy rates at York General, since AMI's takeover, have risen.

What are the differences and advantages between corporate buyout and corporate management without buyout? The significant advantage to selling the hospital is that after the community gains tax revenues from the sale of the hospital, it no longer has to support the hospital through taxes. These previously committed tax funds can be converted to other uses in the community and such use can help to pay for medical care for the indigent.

A corporate management contract can be drawn that allows the community to retain certain controls over the management and policies of the hospital, and a management contract can also be drawn so that it is either a permanent or transitional phase in the operation of your hospital. The tax burden on the community is relieved because the hospital becomes more profitable, but the total burden is not entirely alleviated. However, since the hospital is still community- or county-owned, it remains eligible for government subsidies and certain tax advantages.

Another example of how a hospital management company helped a community concerns Sonoma County, California. In 1975 the county hired National Medical Enterprises (NME) to manage its community hospital. After the first year, NME reduced the county subsidy from $1,757,000 to $865,000—nearly a 50-percent savings for the county! By the end of fiscal year 1981, the hospital was no longer losing money because revenues exceeded expenses by $918,000. Both admissions and occupancy rates increased, and the hospital's cash balance rose significantly, furnishing funds for improvements, additions, and modernization.

Salaries, Benefits, and Employee Tenure

Jessica Townsend in *The New Health Care for Profit*, a booklet published by The Institute of Medicine in the fall of 1983, found that, "In all cases administrators expressed anxiety both about their personal job security and about the tenure of all hospital staff." Benefit packages were mentioned as being high on the list of staff concerns.

Ms. Townsend suggests that job security for the top hospital administrators should be a consideration in the negotiations. In three of the four hospitals studied that were subsequently sold, the corporations did install a new administrator.

Nevertheless, changes in personnel at the top level of administration are accepted by most people as part of doing business with new owners. As the seller, you should be prepared to negotiate with the buyer, as a condition of purchase, to get a certain amount of security for the remainder of the hospital staff. In Ms. Townsend's examples, there was an agreement that all staff would be retained for a certain period of time, ranging from a week to a year. Thereafter, the staff would be judged on competence. One hospital even negotiated an assurance that any staff member judged to be redundant would be offered training for another job in the hospital.

In all but one case, most expressed satisfaction that the sale had resulted in only a low level of staff turnover. "The corporation needs us, and we have good people," was a frequently heard comment.

Benefit packages, although they had been a matter of concern before the sale, turned out to present no problems. Hospital administrators examined the company's benefits in detail and in general found them satisfactory—better than the existing package in some aspects, not as good in others.

Quality of Care

A prime concern, naturally, during a management takeover and resultant changes in hospital personnel is the effect on the quality of care patients will receive. In general, quality of care has actually been improved because of more efficient management, admissions, staff assignments, food service, and distribution of medications.

A comprehensive article in the *New York Times* by N.R. Kleinfeld took a hard look at both sides of the for-profit hospital coin. In discussing quality of care, Kleinfeld reached the following conclusion: "There is no mistaking the health value of the dollars that a [hospital corporation] has to put to work." Peter Frishauf, the editoral director of *Surgical Care Publications* and a long-time observer of the medical scene, adds, "Whether someone likes them or dislikes them for being publicly owned and profitable, the bottom line has to be, do they provide high-quality health care? And the answer, by and large, has to be yes."

Supplies and Services

Investor-owned management companies have cost-effective systems that are available to hospitals for everything from floor cleaning to food service.

Hospital Corporation of America, the largest investor-owned company, has 473 discount supply contracts—covering everything from desks to drugs—to offer individual hospitals, with savings ranging from 15 to 20 percent.

Recently a major hospital in the Midwest was in deep financial trouble with no apparent way out. Rather than sell, the Board of Commissioners decided to hire another medical chain, Hyatt, as consultant. At that time Hyatt owned six hospitals and managed nine.

Hyatt conducted a survey of the hospital, finding the vital medical-records department in chaos and the hospital's operating rooms working at one-third capacity because of a shortage of anesthesiologists. On top of everything else, the hospital had lost $51.3 million due to unpaid bills.

Medical records were quickly brought up to par and the company persuaded the hospital's Board of Commissioners to raise salaries for anesthesiologists to the going level, around $90,000 a year. The hospital was then able to recruit a full complement of anesthesiologists, making it possible to use all 18 operating rooms at capacity. The company collected for the hospital $36 million in unpaid bills, primarily by making patients aware of their eligibility for Medicaid.

Hyatt's reorganization extended to the rest of the hospital. Its 20 kitchens were consolidated into 7, eliminating $700,000 a year in wages, and plans were made to combine several large clinical laboratories. Hyatt earned the hospital $6.2 million a year in interest by slashing in half the time it took to bill Medicaid. The consultants also saved the hospital another $600,000 a year in interest by simply changing the time of day the hospital's daily receipts were picked up and taken to the bank.

Since then the Hyatt hospital operations have been purchased by another firm.

Staffing and Billing

When NME began managing Sonoma County's Community hospital, one of its first actions was to cut the size of the billing office staff from 31 to 18 employees, improving the operation of that office. Staffing efficiency is one area where the investor-owned-for-profit hospital chains excel. Commonly, the personnel-to-patient ratio in government-owned hospitals is about 5.5 to 1, while in for-profit hospitals that ratio is about 2.5 to 1. With labor costs accounting for over half of a hospital's operating expenses, efficient staff use means tremendous savings.

Renovation, Reconstruction, and Equipment

One of the deciding factors in selling a hospital is when the community realizes that it cannot afford to replace or refurbish an obsolete or deteriorating building. Often, even updating aging equipment is out of the financial reach of the community's budget. Turning to a profit-making corporation is becoming the choice, because the corporation has the capital to meet the needs of the community.

A need to replace the hospital plant was the prime reason for the recent sale of two county hospitals, and a guarantee that this would be initiated promptly was made a condition of purchase in both cases. The ability of corporate enterprise to make capital expenditures was a crucial part of the decision to allow the hospitals to be absorbed into the investor-owned sector.

Many of the physicians interviewed in these two purchases wanted to ensure that obsolete equipment would be replaced and that state-of-the-art technology would be introduced.

Several physicians observed that during the first year of corporate operations, new equipment had been bought. In one case, the entire radiology department had been re-equipped and an application for a CAT-scanner had been submitted to the health systems agency.

The corporate purchase of one rural hospital was cited as instrumental in attracting more than 10 physicians to an area reportedly in need of medical manpower. The promise of a new hospital building within two years and the partial renovation of the existing plant were sufficient to attract several specialists, including a cardiologist and neurosurgeon. Today the hospital has new, well-equipped departments to serve these specialists and the community.

A Spectacular Example

Success stories in facilities expansion and redevelopment are taking place in communities all over the country under the direction of hospital management corporations. Hospital Corporation of America (HCA) claims that it can build a hospital 30-40 percent cheaper than a community can by relying on just four builders and prototype designs. National Medical Enterprises, Inc., in a recently published report, showed that when it purchased Doctors Medical Center in Modesto, California, on May 19, 1969, the hospital had 146 beds. Since then, NME has led the facility through the following expansions of beds, services and facilities:

1971: Added 99 medical/surgical beds.

1972: Opened the first emergency room facility in the city of Modesto and the four surrounding counties.

1973: Expanded the radiology department, adding three new rooms.

1974: In January, opened the first noninvasive cardiology lab in Stanislaus County.

1975: In November, opened the first cardiac catheterization lab in the San Joaquin Valley.

1976: In January, introduced CAT-scanning to the Valley.

1977: A cardiac surgery program began with dedicated surgical suites, the first in the Valley.

1978: New 53-bed patient tower opened in May, increasing total capacity to 298 beds, including the first dedicated neurosurgical unit in the San Joaquin Valley.

1979: Initiated outpatient surgery programs as a less costly alternative.

1980: Emergency room was designated first trauma center in seven-county area.

1981: Opened child-care center as an employee benefit during the nursing shortage. Are currently marketing the center to the community, and are planning to expand the number of beds through a certificate of need.

1982: NME acquired 121-bed Modesto City Hospital, which specializes in obstetrics, and has the only neonatal intensive-care unit (ICU) in a four-county area. The facility was acquired at a substantially lower price tag than expanding their current plant and it gave them new service.

Doctors Medical Center now has over 700 employees and annual revenues of $65 million. Outside of the Gallo Winery in Modesto, it is the largest employer in a city of 125,000 people. What has been accomplished at Doctors Medical Center can be accomplished at other locations as well.

Richard Threlkeld of ABC's *World News Tonight* provides a concise summary of this issue in the following excerpt from a story he did from Scottsdale, Arizona, about privatization of public services.

"In Corsicana, Texas, the Navarro County Hospital was growing old, losing money and about to lose its accreditation. It would have cost the county $12 million to fix it up, too much for the taxpayers.

"The Hospital Corporation of America is building a brand-new private hospital, right next to the old one. It'll handle Medicare and charity patients and charge the rates the county decides on. It can do that and make a profit because it deals in quantity. It runs 350 hospitals like this one. The old county hospital was costing the taxpayers about $50,000 a year. The new private hospital will be paying $316,000 a year in taxes.

"What's the point? Simply that in serving the public there is nothing sacred about either public service or private enterprise. It all depends on the enterprise. In Corsicana and Boston and here in Scottsdale, they applied a little ingenuity to do what's best. In the competition between business and government to see who can best do the public's work cheaply, efficiently and fairly, the real winners are bound to be the taxpayers."

VII

CONTRACT SERVICES FOR WASTEWATER TREATMENT

Coordinated by John A. Sedwick from contributions by the staff of Envirotech

In *practically all of 50 cities studied, local officials have improved their cost-effectiveness by contracting out.*

A city faces fines. And a sewer connection ban that will shut down new development. Worse . . . influent loadings are increasing to 20 percent above capacity. While the plant is aging.

This seems like desperation time to many government officials.

But it is not uncommon for a private contractor to turn that around and bring a town into compliance in a year. Sometimes six months.

This extremely useful chapter, assembled by John A. Sedwick from the Envirotech staff, shows what a full contract operation is. It lays out detailed steps for searching and selecting a good contractor, writing a good contract, and for supervising the chosen contractor in action.

The chapter excels as a tool for you in enlisting community support for contracting out and educating your colleagues and constituents. A comprehensive question-and-answer section anticipates all the usual questions. For example:

What about present municipal-plant employees?

Do we lose control?

How evaluate contractors?

What do we do if contractor does not perform?

Contractor relations with EPA?

Who pays EPA fines?

What if contractor walks out?

A very useful appendix contains samples: request for proposals; contract inclusions; and an excellent case history segment.

The great effect of the chapter is projecting the conviction that contract water-treatment supplies:

- stability of expenditure
- shift of accountability to contractor
- improved relations with state and federal government

This is the only chapter in this handbook prepared by a private company. However, it avoids self-serving information and sticks to operational information. John Sedwick, coordinator of the chapter, works for Envirotech Operating Services. He was a major contributor to the EPA manual on Contract Operators, published in 1982.

—The Editors

Since initiation of the Clean Water Act in 1972, Congress has appropriated over $37 billion to upgrade or build new wastewater treatment facilities. The legislative goals were to restore polluted waters to a quality that allow for the protection and propagation of fish, shellfish, wildlife, and recreational use. Another goal was to eliminate all discharges of pollutants into the nation's navigable waters.

In 1980, a General Accounting Office (GAO) report indicated significant noncompliance with National Pollutant Discharge Elimination System (NPDES) permit limits at major municipal facilities. This finding was further confirmed by GAO in 1983 with over 30 percent of a random-sample of major municipal dischargers found to be in significant noncompliance with their permit limits.

One major reason for this noncompliance can be attributed to the fact that, during the last decade, wastewater treatment facilities have become more complex and sophisticated while the availability of skilled management, supervisory, maintenance, and operating personnel has not expanded at the same rate.

Municipalities have spent millions on advanced treatment equipment while failing to provide adequate funding for operator training programs. Within the new facilities, the advent of more complex technology without concomitant upgrading of staff has resulted in excessive rates of operator turnover. All too often, competent people who have successfully operated a primary treatment plant have been thrown into an upgraded facility without proper training or hands-on experience. The end result is poor performance, followed by poor morale—which only compounds the performance problem.

Inadequate experience and training, frequently because of insufficient budgets, are often manifested, for example, in premature or needless deterioration of equipment due to poorly conceived and administered maintenance programs. Thus, the inexperienced or ill-trained manager is the unwitting cause of less than capable performance by both staff and plant equipment.

Generally speaking, modern wastewater treatment facilities can and will perform to design capabilities when staffed by experienced, well-trained operating, management, and line personnel. Rather than placing the blame for inadequate performance on equipment or plant design, or insufficient funds due to municipal budget constraints, troubled municipalities may be able to correct operational problems by securing assistance from the private sector through contracted services. In so doing, it is important that both the problems and the desired scope of services required be clearly defined beforehand. For example, some of the objectives essential to a good plant operation and maintenance are:

1. Plant efficiency and effluent quality;
2. Quality plant and equipment maintenance;
3. Good employee morale and low turnover;

4. Planned program to correct plant deficiencies;
5. Stabilized costs of operation and maintenance.

While there are numerous individual operations assistance services available through which these objectives might be achieved (i.e., operator training, process optimization and assistance, new plant start-up supervision and maintenance systems and service) a full service operation-and-maintenance contract provides the most comprehensive program in a single cost-effective package.

What Is a Full Contract Operation and Maintenance Program?

Contract operations and maintenance are services performed by a private firm which signs an agreement with a municipality typically for five years, sometimes longer, wherein that firm takes full responsibility for the operation and maintenance of a wastewater treatment facility. Operating under a fixed dollar budget and guaranteeing plant performance and effluent quality, the private contractor is responsible for payment of all normal and routine costs associated with the facility with the exception of major capital expenditures. In addition, the employees of the plant become employees of the private contracting firm with benefits programs typically equivalent to what they received from the municipality.

Contract operation is becoming an increasingly accepted and popular alternative for municipalities across the country. It is not a new concept; there are at least 50 municipalities within the United States currently contracting out their wastewater treatment plant. In essentially all cases, contract operations have proven to be more cost-effective to a municipality than previous municipal operations.

Why Contract?

While *cost saving* is frequently expressed as the initial motivation, municipalities considering private-sector operations and maintenance contracts in reality generally have a variety of other equally significant problems. The following are some of the typical problems confronting the community:

- *Start-up of a new complex facility* without sufficient technical capabilities.
- *Shortage of trained operating personnel* leading to poor plant operations.
- *Effluent violations* resulting in regulatory actions such as: fines; building moratoriums; state/federal funding withheld.
- *Odors* causing a public nuisance.
- *Poor equipment maintenance* resulting in deterioration of capital investment.
- *Personnel/union problems* contributing to poor morale and high employee turnover.
- *Public dissatisfaction with odor or effluent problems* creating political pressures and adverse publicity.
- *High unstable cost of operation* causing inordinate increases in sewer user fees.

What Is Included in an Operations and Maintenance Contract?

When a private firm assumes operations and maintenance responsibility for a municipal facility, the contractual obligations generally provide for the following:

- *Guaranteed plant performance* with the contractor paying fines for effluent violations.
- A wide range of *technical expertise and backup* to minimize such operating problems as odors, process upsets, excessive energy consumption.
- An extensive set of *training programs* to improve the capabilities of the personnel resulting in improved efficiency and advancement opportunities and a safe working environment.
- Dedicated staffs for *community relations* to minimize or eliminate any potential problems between citizen groups and City Hall.

- *Reduced administrative burden* on municipal management allows more time for focusing on key issues, other priority operations, and planning for future growth rather than involvement in day-to-day operations.
- *A stabilized budget.* Typically the price under a contract of this nature is adjusted only for change in scope of services (e.g., significantly increased flows) and changes in nationally recognized indexes (e.g., Consumer Price Index). This budget commitment can further minimize cost increases and, hence, user rates. In constant dollars, the program costs should increase only for significant increases in flows and loadings resulting from the growth of the city.
- *Improved technology such as computerized process control and maintenance management systems.* Leading firms possess these capabilities which a city could not economically develop because these firms have been able to spread development costs over many plants.
- *Elimination of employee-relations problems* and related issues for the city. The contract operator should assume full responsibility.
- *Higher quality of operations* through use of sophisticated operational technology, professional expertise, and proven management systems and procedures.
- Because of this expertise, further *cost savings* should be offered through a shared cost savings program where the city and the contractor split additional cost savings that develop throughout the life of the contract, further minimizing potential rate increases.

Potential Concerns and Issues

While many cities are quite pleased with contract operations, there are a number of questions that can reasonably be asked, answers for which must be satisfactorily provided before all parties to the decision can feel comfortable. Some of the more common questions and answers are listed below:

Q. What happens to the current employees, especially if the contract operator wants to reduce the staff?

A. It is possible that staff reduction could occur overtime. While not always the case, even if a reduction is recommended, the city and the private contractor would develop a joint program for staff reduction, probably over a given period of time, to allow attrition and relocation to other departments within the city to effect a smooth and nondisruptive change. Potential staff level is one of a number of issues that points to the need for the private firm to have a highly qualified, dedicated employee relations staff who can address the concerns and well-being of employees, and a proven record of successful assumption of operations and employees.

Q. Why can't we do the job as cheaply as an outside firm who will surely be making a profit as well?

A. A large firm will have a high level of expertise based on the necessarily broader range of experience. It should have more qualified people, particularly in support positions, to assist in problem-solving and systems development since a larger firm can spread its costs over many plants, a luxury a single-plant operator does not enjoy. Further, a private firm (because of a variety of incentives not open to municipalities) may have higher productivity per employee. A larger firm can also enjoy economies of scale through expanded purchasing capability.

Q. Why not use a consultant firm to show us where to cut costs?

A. Without ongoing, on-site management committed to changes and new systems and procedures, any benefits so derived may be short-lived. Further, some firms use proprietary systems only in plants where they have long-term contracts. The ongoing, shared cost-savings programs are less likely to be realized after the expert contractor is no longer available. Other benefits, such as effluent guarantees, fixed dollar-budget commitment, liability protection, backup technical support, and employee and community relations skills are lost as well if the contractor is only involved in short-term consultation.

Q. How is the city protected if the contractor fails to perform?

A. Typically, the contract with the firm stipulates that the agreement can be terminated if the contractor fails to perform and includes a phase-out provision for the city to have the right to hire the plant employees. In addition, the contract operations firm provides liability protection, effluent fine coverage, assumes responsibility for its negligence and posts a performance bond. When selecting a firm, the underlying size, asset base, and demonstrated track record are essential factors of protection which should be considered.

Q. If the contractor arbitrarily decides to leave, how can we operate the plant?

A. The contract should (and generally does) specify that *either* party can only terminate for cause. Realistically, the unilateral termination by the contractor would create sufficiently severe repercussions in that its reputation would be permanently damaged. Posting a performance bond is another safeguard. This is just one of many reasons the selected contractor should be a well-established, financially sound firm, committed to the wastewater industry.

Q. Do we lose control?

A. The city does not lose control. The selection of the most qualified contractor is probably the surest guarantee of a successful program. But the contract itself can be written to ensure that the city retains control. The city should have one of its employees serve as a contract administrator to monitor performance. Performance would be monitored by a reporting system that the contractor would be required to provide. In addition, the contractor's on-site manager will function as a city staff member. Rather than losing control, the city is actually acquiring additional resources and augmenting its staff.

Key Benefits of Contract
Operations and Maintenance

A significant benefit accruing to the municipality under private-sector contract operations and maintenance is the ability to shift accountability for wastewater quality. Through the assignment to the contractor of the obligation for both guaranteed performance and a share of noncompliance liability, the municipality can enjoy the inherently more efficient performance and expertise found in successful free enterprise, while, at the same time, achieving stability in the expenditure of public monies. This efficiency also extends to the original capital investment made for equipment and the physical plant as well.

Superior performance on a continuous basis with a well-trained, certified staff backed by technical support, improved laboratory analysis, data collection, and reporting is ensured. Further, municipal officials and staff will be free to concentrate on new challenges while maintaining improved relationships with state and federal regulatory agencies.

Important Considerations

When a municipality is considering a full-contract operations-and-management program, it should be recognized as a major undertaking. Accordingly, the entire contracting procedure should be well thought out and planned in advance.

Preparatory to selecting a contractor, the municipality should:

1. Make sure that the governing body—city council, district, or authority—has endorsed the concept.
2. Review labor agreements to make sure that private-sector contracting is possible.
3. Establish a written procurement procedure and timetable.
4. Define the scope of services that will meet the city's needs.
5. Conduct legal counsel review of the prospective contract's terms and conditions.
6. Inform affected current plant personnel of actions taken and assure them their best interests will be addressed. This is very important. Fear of change may have a very negative impact.

The municipality should also recognize that no responsible contractor will absorb capital costs for new equipment that is the property of the city, assume unlimited liability and risk, or guarantee performance beyond the physical capability of the treatment system and the laws of nature.

Selecting an Operations-and-Maintenance Contractor

The municipality should recognize that an operations-and-maintenance firm is a professional service and, therefore, does not require competitive bidding. The contractor should be selected through a preselection process that results in a negotiated contract with the contractor who can best meet the municipality's specific needs. Because of the multiplicity of skills and technical support required for a successful program, "low bidders" often do not represent the most cost-effective alternative long term.

In order to be selected, a firm should be able to demonstrate the following:

1. A minimum of five years' experience in full contract operations-and-maintenance program with proven successful performance.
2. Proven experience in operating facilities of similar complexity or size.
3. Proven financial stability and commitment to the business.
4. Ability to post a performance bond for the full contract amount.
5. A list of references identifying all current customers under contract for full operations and maintenance (O&M). Such a list should include name, telephone numbers of responsible parties, and a description of respective plant sizes and complexities. References should be screened.
6. Proven technical and management backup expertise as demonstrated by an organizational chart and personnel résumés.
7. Full-time, on-staff labor relations specialist, a critical issue for continuity in plant personnel.

With these and other qualifications, the city can derive substantial benefits from contract operations and maintenance while minimizing or eliminating pitfalls.

Steps in Selecting an O&M Contractor

1. On a confidential basis, determine if there are any unforeseen and unanticipated concerns from the administration and staff in pursuing this opportunity.
2. Identify prospective contractors.
3. Form a selection committee and establish an objective method to evaluate the various firms using a selection criteria such as discussed above.
4. Develop and send out a request for qualifications.
5. From the responses, develop a short list of two or three of the most qualified firms. (Sample evaluation form is attached as Appendix A)
   (Note: In contracting for a professional service, a city may proceed from Step 5 to select the most qualified firm and negotiate only with that firm for the provision of services it seeks. An alternative is to proceed with Step 6, a Request for Proposal.)
6. Develop a Request for Proposal. (Sample attached as Appendix B)
7. Assemble information the contractor's will need to develop a priced proposal (information needs list attached as Appendix C).
8. Send out a Request for Proposal, the response for which would include a scope of services, performance expectation, employee package, price and reasons why the firm is qualified based upon experience and qualifications.
9. Receive and evaluate proposals. When evaluating two or more proposals, it should be done on an apples-to-apples basis with a clear idea of the specific services and benefits included in each proposal.
10. Interview firms and visit reference cities.
11. Based on the previously determined selection criteria, select one firm with whom to negotiate.
12. Negotiate contract.
13. Obtain council approval.
14. Contractor to assume plant operations and maintenance.

Selecting a quality contractor with a proven successful track record is the key to achieving the maximum benefit from a private sector service alternative. Keep in mind that the full operations and maintenance contract is a long-term relationship of five years or more. It is important that the contractor can work well with the municipal staff, become part of the community, and serve as a good neighbor. Due to this long-term relationship, it is also important that the contract be sufficiently comprehensive so as to avoid confusion and misunderstandings by either party. An unbiased, objective, and thorough procurement process is the best guarantee for achieving the anticipated benefits of this type program.

The Municipal Official

Demands on municipal officers and resources continue to escalate. The public requires municipal management to effectively provide increasing services and at reasonable cost. Use of private-sector organizations to assist in achieving those objectives can be a productive management alternative.

Contract operations and maintenance of wastewater treatment facilities allow municipalities to benefit from effective specialized expertise at a fixed cost without diverting resources from other essential services.

Case Histories

Facility: 13 MGD and 4 MGD municipal wastewater treatment plants; 4 MGD industrial pretreatment facility, on-site laboratory.

Service Scope: Complete operation and maintenance of the three facilities and industrial monitoring program.

Description and Accomplishments—No. 1

The contractor began operations during the summer of 1978. At that time, the city faced both potential fines and a sewer connection ban by the state regulatory agency. Compounding the problem, loadings were increasing substantially while the plant was consistently failing to meet its discharge standards. For four years, the 13-MGD activated sludge facility with thermal solids conditioning, extractors, and a multiple hearth furnace had been trying to cope with heavy industrial loads, internal solids build-up, and frequent equipment disrepair. Under the contractor's supervision, effluent compliance was achieved within six months despite the high industrial loads, 20 percent above design capacity.

A computerized process control and monitoring system developed by the contractor was utilized to monitor and analyze process data. This analysis allowed the contractor's technical staff to understand process dynamics and develop a strategy for achieving effluent quality.

Subsequently, under the contract program, the city commissioned an industrial pretreatment lagoon and reactivated the 4-MGD secondary treatment plant. This three-facility interrelated system has been successfully operated by the contractor and the contract scope expanded accordingly.

The 4-MGD facility provides secondary treatment and discharges process solids to the 13-MGD facility for treatment and disposal. Process control and operational expertise have eliminated the severe odor problems and prevented filamentous bulking that were previously experienced. The contractor also eliminated upsets at the 13-MGD facility by effective management of the 4-MGD sludge quality and transfer.

Under the contract operation, the heat treatment process was operationally eliminated and programs initiated with local industry to help find a cost-effective disposal option for pulp and canning wastes.

The contractor works closely with the city, local industry, and design consultants to insure a cost-effective pretreatment program through an extensive industrial sampling, lagoon monitoring, and process control management program.

The contractor is currently participating with city staff and the design engineer in planning cost-effective modifications and a programmed expansion to meet the city's treatment needs for the future. Recently, the city voted unanimously to renew the contract for a period of ten years—an industry first.

Facility: 8.4-MGD pure oxygen municipal wastewater treatment plant; nine pump stations, on-site laboratory.

Service
Scope: Complete operation and maintenance of facility and four pump stations.

Description and Accomplishments— No. 2

The contractor assumed operational responsibility of this three-year-old 8.4-MGD pure oxygen treatment plant on November 1, 1980. At the time of contract commencement, the city was facing regulatory agency fines, imposition of a sewer hookup ban, and numerous odor complaints from local residents. In addition, the Economic Development Administration (EDA) was withholding $1.7 million of funding for construction of an industrial complex in the city due to the chronic effluent violation situation.

Within the first six months of this six-year contract, the contractor brought the facility into NPDES compliance for the first time in its history through use of its backup technical support staff, implementation of its computer process management system, and implementation of maintenance and training programs. Seven months after contract commencement, the entire facility was opened for a tour by city and state officials as well as the public (with over 500 persons participating). The contractor's program at the city received praise from municipal and regulatory officials. Within the first year, the EDA released all of the $1.7 million in withheld funding, allowing completion of the vital new industrial complex.

Despite recent additions of new toxic industrial discharges to the treatment facility, the contractor has maintained its outstanding NPDES performance record at a fixed price to the city which is less than the original cost estimate for continued city operation. The contractor's industrial monitoring program is recognized by regulatory officials as one of the first such successful programs.

Facility: 5.6-MGD municipal wastewater treatment plant; four (4) pump stations, on-site laboratory.

Service
Scope: Complete operation and maintenance of facility and pump stations.

Description and Accomplishments—No. 3

The contractor assumed operation of this 5.5-MGD secondary plant in February 1979. In 1978, the city faced potential enforcement actions because of numerous odor complaints emanating from the facility and its secondary oxidation pond. A lack of maintenance compounded the issue by resulting in extensive equipment problems and rising repair costs.

The advent of California's Proposition 13 added one more complication by placing tight funding constraints on the city. During the first year of the five-year agreement, the contractor met effluent standards, eliminated the odor problems, and returned the plant to a stable operation and maintenance mode—all within a fixed, guaranteed budget that did not exceed the city's wastewater treatment budget.

Subsequently, the facility experienced a "once-in-100-years" storm that knocked out power and threatened basic plant integrity. The contractor's on-site team, augmented by the regional staff and other contractor specialists, responded to protect the plant property, and maintained treatment. The contractor received special recognition from the city for this effort and expertise. On one occasion, a design defect in a new plant pump station had caused dry well flooding and partial loss of plant operability. Again, the contractor's on-site personnel and backup specialists responded to remedy the problem and provide major repairs at substantial savings to the city.

Today, the contractor is working closely with the city and its design engineer on a facility expansion and water reclamation facility. The contractor will be responsible for the new facility start-up and integration into the existing program. Also, the city recently voted unanimously to renew the contract for an additional five years.

The facility continues to consistently meet effluent quality under the contractor's program.

Facility: 15-MGD advanced wastewater treatment plant; four sewage pump stations, energy recovery facility, on-site laboratory.

Service Scope: Complete operation and maintenance of facility, pump stations, and industrial monitoring program.

Description and Accomplishments—No. 4

Through an agreement initiated in 1974 at the district's then secondary treatment facility, the contractor solved odor and air pollution problems. The district's new $52 million tertiary facility, started up by the contractor in 1977, now represents the contract facility. Designed to serve a major brewery, an Air Force Base and two cities, the plant's performance is of extreme importance in protecting a marshland that represents one-fifth of the total national wildlife refuge preserve for North America and provides water reuse for nearby agricultural activities.

The contractor has consistently achieved effluent quality, commencing with the fourth day of plant start-up and, most notably, maintained this record during a $19-million facility expansion completed in 1982.

The contractor worked closely with the district engineer, design consultants, and contractors to develop a successful program which ensures an operable design and on-going cost-effective plant operation. The facility expansion included anaerobic digestors to replace aerobic digestors, plate and frame presses, and engine-generator sets to produce electric power using methane as fuel.

The filter press building is now the model installation in the United States and the energy recovery system is fully operational, producing 4,000 KWH/day.

The contract has been renewed twice and incentive savings programs were added at the second renewal to share in savings and hold cost increases to less than inflationary rates. The district has gained incentive savings of more than $100,000 during the past two years of this program while O&M cost increases have been kept below actual inflation rates.

APPENDIX A

Sample Contractor Evaluation Form

CITY OF _____

EVALUATION OF CONTRACT AND MAINTENANCE PROPOSALS

Name of Firm

Evaluation Criteria	Total Points Per Item	1	2	3	4	5	6
A. Proven successful performance in plants of similar size, complexity, and treatment requirements (for a minimum of five years) located in the United States as supported by firm's references. (Areas for proven successful performance include: effluent quality, odor control, employee training programs, maintenance performance, laboratory quality assurance, and client relations)	45						

CITY OF _____

EVALUATION OF CONTRACT AND MAINTENANCE PROPOSALS

Evaluation Criteria	Total Points Per Item	Name of Firm					
		1	2	3	4	5	6
B. Financial stability and ability to post a performance bond for the full five-year contract amount. Wholly owned subsidiaries allowed to list only their own value—not that of the parent company.	20						
C. Proven technical and management backup expertise as demonstrated by an organization chart, personnel resumes, and documentable performance.	15						
D. Provision of a formal safety program backed by a record of demonstrable success.	15						
E. Provision of a formal maintenance management system proven over at least five years of actual Contract O&M experience.	20						
F. Ability and willingness to comply with the provisions described in the request for proposal.	15						

(continued)

G.	Demonstrated full-time employment of a labor relations specialist with expertise in personnel/labor negotiations proven over a minimum ten-year period.	10
H.	Provision of a computer process management system which offers proven performance under actual operating conditions.	10
I.	O&M Contractor should not be owned by a Waste Water Treatment Plant design firm to avoid inherent conflict of interest.	10
J.	Provision of references identifying *all* current customers *under contract for full O&M.* List to include name/telephone number of responsible parties and a description of respective plant sizes/complexities.	10
K.	Proven experience of successfully taking new plants and plant expansions through start-up operations and modifications and demonstrated ability to work with independent design consultants and construction contractors.	20
L.	Demonstrated industrial monitoring and waste-water treatment capability with proven cooperative ability with client and industrial discharger.	10
	TOTAL POINTS	200

APPENDIX B
REQUEST FOR PROPOSAL
FOR Operation and
Maintenance
of the Wastewater
Treatment plant

The city of _____ is soliciting proposals for the complete operation and maintenance of its wastewater treatment facility.

Description of Facilities

(Clearly describe the facilities, including pump stations, if applicable, which will be the responsiblity of the contractor)

Scope of Services to Be Provided

The scope of services contained in the proposal shall include all operation, maintenance, and laboratory testing activities as required to operate the treatment plant in a manner that complies with all legal and regulatory requirements *for a minimum period of five (5) years.* These shall include:

1. Provision of a sufficient number of qualified employces, who meet applicable state certification requirements, to operate and maintain the treatment plant in a professional manner.
2. Provision of all wages, salaries, utilities and consumables, such as fuel and lubricants, incurred in normal treatment plant operations.
3. Provision of all routine and normal maintenance of plant equipment and grounds.
4. Provision of a proven professional preventive maintenance management and scheduling system.
5. Provision of additional management, technical, administrative, and labor relations expertise to augment plant personnel.
6. Provision of on-going training for plant personnel.

7. Provision of a process control management system.
8. Provision of laboratory testing as required for process control and compliance with the National Pollutant Discharge Elimination System (NPDES) permit reporting requirements.
9. Provision of management services including preparation, maintenance, and submission of all required monitoring and operating reports.
10. Provision of a written guarantee of effluent quality.
11. Provision of regulatory fine liability in accordance with an amount and terms to be negotiated with the city.
12. Provision of public liability insurance in an amount not less than $1,000,000 combined single limits for personal injury and/or property damage.
13. Provision of liability protection to the city for damages caused by the willful and intentional neglect of the contractor.
14. Provision of a lump sum price subject to change only due to changes in the scope of services or changes in established cost indexes.
15. Provision of an effective odor abatement program.
16. Provision for contract termination based upon proven breach of contract by city or vendor.

Hours of Operation

(Describe the hours of operation required)

Equipment and Service to Be Provided by the City

(If applicable, describe any services, equipment or vehicles which may be provided by the city)

Contractor Selection

Based upon an evaluation of the proposals received, as well as an associated interview, one contractor will be selected to negotiate a contract. Selection and ranking of the firms shall be in accordance with the following criteria:

1. A minimum of five years experience in full contract

operation and maintenance with proven, successful performance.

2. Proven, successful experience in operating facilities of similar complexity or size under a full O&M contract containing written effluent guarantee, fixed price (with scope or indices change allowances), with a 5-year contractual commitment.

3. Proven financial stability and corporate commitment to the business.

4. Proven ability to post a performance bond for the full five-year contract amount.

5. A list of references identifying *all* current customers *under contract for full O&M* with your firm. List will include name/telephone numbers of responsible parties and a description of respective plant sizes/complexities.

6. Proven technical and management backup expertise as demonstrated by an organization chart and personnel resumes.

7. Demonstrated full-time employment of a labor relations specialist with proven expertise in personnel/labor negotiations.

8. Demonstrated ability and willingness to comply with the provisions described under the scope of services above.

9. Proven full-time safety program.

10. Formal proven preventive maintenance system.

All proposals shall include sufficient information to evaluate the firm based upon the above criteria.

Schedule of Events

All proposals shall be submitted in triplicate to _____ by no later than _____.

The proposed schedule for selection, negotiation and service initiation is as follows:

Item	Date
Forward RFPs to selected firms	
Receive proposals	

Review proposals

Oral interviews

Evaluation and ranking of firms

Selection of firm for negotiations
Initiate negotiations

Complete negotiations and obtain approval of
negotiated contract

Initiate service

Inspection of Facilities and Data Provision

Your firm shall be allowed to inspect the applicable facilities in accordance with an agreed-upon schedule. Sufficient data will be provided for preparation of a responsive proposal including, but not limited to, the following:

1. *Plant Design Capacity.* Flow (mgd), BOD (lbs/day or mg/l) and SS (lbs/day or mg/l).
2. *Existing Plant Loadings.* Flow, BOD, SS
3. *Monthly Monitoring Reports.* Showing influent and effluent quality (BOD and SS) for last 36 months.
4. *Flow Sheet/Plant Layout.* Reproduced from construction drawings or O&M manual.
5. *Discharge Requirements.* Copy of current NPDES permit.
6. *Current Budget.* Detailed by line item cost. Identifying line item costs which would not be the responsibility of the O&M contractor.
7. *Financial Statement.* Actual versus budgeted expenditures by line item for the current and two previous years.
8. *Industrial Wastes.* Listed by type of wastes and quantity. Identifying major industrial dischargers.
9. *Union Agreement.* A copy of the current union agreement, if applicable.
10. *Employee Compensation.* An employee salary schedule, description of benefits and cost of benefits, retirement plan and employee/employer contribution rates.
11. *Organization Chart.* Indicating current staffing.
12. *Safety Program.* Occupational and Safety Hazards Administration (OSHA) inspection reports.

APPENDIX C
PLANT EVALUATION
INFORMATION NEEDS

1. *Major Problems.* Please describe those problems you would like resolved through contract O&M services, i.e., chronic noncompliance odors, equipment maintenance, labor relations, annual budgeting.
2. *Scope of Service.* List the specific facilities to be considered, i.e., wastewater treatment plant, water treatment plant, pump stations, distribution systems, collection system, and/or outfall pipes.
3. *Plant Design Capacity.* Flow (mgd), BOD (lbs/day or mg/l), and SS (lbs/day or mg/l).
4. *Existing Plant Loadings.* Flow, BOD, SS
5. *Monthly Monitoring Reports.* Show influent and effluent quality (BOD and SS) for last 12 months.
6. *Flow Sheet/Plant Layout.* Reproduce from construction drawings or O&M manual.
7. *Discharge Requirements.* Copy of current NPDES permit.
8. *Current budget.* Detailed by line item cost. Identify line item costs which would not be the responsibility of the O&M contractor.
9. *Financial Statement.* Show actual versus budgeted expenditures by line item for the current and two previous years.
10. *Industrial Wastes.* List type of wastes and quantity. Identify major industrial dischargers.
11. *Union Agreement.* Provide a copy of the current union agreement, if applicable.
12. *Employee Compensation.* Provide an employee salary schedule, description of benefits and cost of benefits, retirement plan and employee/employer contribution rates.
13. *Organization Chart.* Indicate current staffing.
14. Safety Program. Copy OSHA inspection reports.

VIII

DAY CARE

by Robert L. Woodson
President, National Center for
Neighborhood Enterprise

The need for child care has come on with such speed that in one decade, 1970-1980, the percentage of women in the work force wih children aged six or under leaped from a third to nearly half. In nearly every neighborhood, there are capable people eager to furnish the needed day care. But rushing in to supervise them are formidable city and state bureaucracies with such ponderous regulations and paperwork that they defeat day care.

With taxes commanding approximately 40 percent of a household's income, it becomes practically imperative for the lady of the house to work outside. That creates the massive demand for child care . . . not storage . . . but *care.* Care involves tenderness, love, and establishment of life values in our next generation of Americans.

That . . . makes it outrank all the previous services in this volume.

How do we best supply that?

Local officials will soon find their constituencies looking to them for breakthrough help in this service.

Robert L. Woodson is president of National Center for Neighborhood Enterprise, 1367 Connecticut Avenue, N.W.,

Washington, D.C. 20036. He is also an adjunct fellow of American Enterprise Institute and has been director of that institute's Neighborhood Revitalization Project. He has been a fellow of the National Endowment for Humanities and director of the Administration of Justice Division of National Urban League. As a younger man, he served in several social work fields involving child care.

In addition to his professional work, Robert Woodson has written extensively on the welfare of children in such leading newspapers as *The New York Times, The Washington Post, The Philadelphia Inquirer.*

Perceptive public officials planning forward to prioritize the problems of the near future will find child day care ascendant. The need may not have become intensive in your particular community yet, but it probably will. The urgency behind the drive for good child day care is that the parents' ability to make a living is dependent upon it. That gives the problem number one rank.

A popular misconception is that child care is mostly needed in poor or welfare communities. The reverse is the case. Good income families are the biggest users of child day care.

—The Editors

Despite the need for a full partnership between the public and private sectors to ensure increased quality alternatives in child care services, day care is and will remain a very personalized consumer activity. Family day care homes and, increasingly, for-profit private centers that can be more responsive to the individualized needs of parents will offer the most viable day care options for the many diverse life-styles of working families.

• In October 1974, a small number of licensed day care operators in California formed the Oakland Licensed Day Care Association, a nonprofit corporation, to work towards increased uniformity in the interpretation of county and state child care legislation. Because of the flexibility of many of these homes, the Association has for the past decade served thousands of families. Now comprising some 153 family day care homes, Association members offer customer families flexible hours, at least from 7 a.m. until 7 p.m. with many providing around-the-clock and weekend care. Other unique features of the Association include a toy and book lending library, a credit union, group insurance and notary services.

• In Augusta, Maine, one enterprising woman opened up a day-care program in a seniors nursing home. But in spite of this creative combination of both child and elderly care services, she must respond to ongoing—and seemingly unnecessary flak—from state and city licensing authorities relative to the "potential" risks of mixing chldren and elderly citizens in a single environment. A similar program is working quite successfully in El Paso.

• A District of Columbia woman who has run her day care center out of her home in a residential section of the city since 1978 faces jail unless she closes her doors. Despite the quality care she is providing to 12 school-aged children, including several handicapped, city officials cited her for zoning violations. Not only does this woman manage to provide an adequate income for herself, many of the parents of the children in her care do not feel they can find the same quality care at affordable rates elsewhere in the city.

• A Denver, Colorado, entrepreneur, because of the large number of single parents with children in his neighborhood, bought an apartment complex for such parents and runs an innovative day care program on the property. Parent fees cover the cost of the facility and the children are cared for right in the neighborhood.

• Another enterprising mother in Kansas City, Kansas, capitalized on the model cities designation of her city and started a day care center in her neighborhood with a modest SBA loan.

• A low-income inner city Des Moines, Iowa, program, which operates on a shoestring budget, offers care for over 300 children, ranging in age from 2 to 13 years, from 6 a.m. to 1:30 a.m. seven days a week. Its success, according to its director, is a direct result of "heavy" parental involvement. Parents are expected to sponsor fundraising events, serve on policymaking boards and lobby on behalf of the organization. A number of parents of the children have moved from welfare into paid staff jobs because day care freed them to find work and accept jobs.

The Child Care Situation

By 1990, as many as 20 million children under the age of five will need day care. Yet, despite a documented and ever-increasing need for child-care services across all income groups as well as an overabundance of related state-level regulations of such services, there is a critical shortage of quality child care options for those who need them. And although there seems to be a trend toward private businesses picking up the slack via employer-supported programs and centers, only very large companies can afford the benefit. In fact, there are a number of tax and other fiscal *disincentives* for employer-owned and operated centers.

The reality is that privatization alone is no panacea. Indeed, privatization and its sister, industrialization, particularly in the context of Western democracies, are mother to the welfare state. And, as a result, the two—privatization and the welfare state—are also partners in the notion that the state has some responsibility for caring for its members, particularly its poor and disenfranchised.

Yet, as in many morally inspired partnerships between the private and public sectors, the private sector either dropped out or was smothered by its more zealous public counterpart with the result that social service delivery has become the exclusive purview of a vast professional bureaucracy whose unique function is to keep its citizens dependent.

The economic costs alone of maintaining this state-enforced system of professional service providers is staggering. But more important, such a system of service delivery exacerbates the very problems it was designed to remedy. This Catch-22 is increasingly apparent in the delivery of child-care services in the United States.

Regulating Child Care

During the past three decades, there has been a dramatic fourfold increase in working mothers with children aged six and under—from 12 percent in 1947 to 50 percent in 1982. For mothers of children under age 18, the U.S. Bureau of Labor Statistics reports an increase in the labor force from 40 percent in 1970 to nearly 60 percent in 1983. *Today, in short, more than half of our nation's children have working parents.*

TABLE 1
Percent of Women with Children Aged Six and Under in the Work Force

Year	Percent*
1950	13.6
1960	20.2
1970	32.2
1980	46.7

*Married and once-married women.

Source: U.S. Bureau of the Census, *Trends in Child Care Arrangements of Working Mothers* (Washington, D.C.: U.S. Government Printing Office, 1982).

Moreover, in this country, when we speak of child care, we are talking about much more than day care for children of working parents. Currently, the definition of child care also includes:

• Day care for children in abuse or neglect situations;
• Child welfare;
• Pre-school enrichment programs for the low-income, e.g., Head Start;
• Child health and nutrition programs and others.

As a result, all-encompassing government regulations, whether appropriate or not, generally exist across all these programs.

Government policies and programs are often fragmented by such factors as income, age, neighborhood, and profit versus nonprofit status. This fragmentation can result in the complete breakdown of supportive systems such as day care, despite the necessity. Also, because there are numerous government agencies responsible for different pieces of legislation, regulations, monitoring, or funding relative to day care, the resultant process is little more than a maze of duplicative, contradictory, time-consuming, and unnecessary paperwork. In Washington, D.C., for example, there are 57 required forms for day-care licensing and monitoring. The person who is good at handling children is not expert at handling paper.

Another major problem is the myriad of regulations that are neither capable of being monitored nor applicable to the *variety* of day care programs. The results are inflated costs for parents and inadequate salaries with little or no fringe benefits for staff and/or providers. An offshoot of this problem, of course, is an extremely high-turnover rate among providers, to the ultimate detriment of our children.

Day-care subsidy programs are based on income levels that are often unrealistic. If, for example, a parent exceeds the allowable income level of a particular program, then he or she is dropped from that program. Thus, the current system locks people into being poor by forcing them, in some cases, to turn down raises or promotions. Such subsidy programs are contrary to the goals of Title XX, which was designed to sustain and maintain self-sufficiency.

Many states have centers and homes that are 100-percent federally funded. When a parent exceeds the eligibility level, the child must leave the facility. This type of policy may not only be very traumatic to a child but contradicts the intent of many regulations.

Complicating the issue of regulatory monitoring of day care is the inconsistency in "intent" of policies, that is, some regulations have a distinct bias toward nonprofit programs while others are designed to facilitate profit-making entities. For example, for-profit centers may be ineligible for the food program subsidies unless they are sponsored by a nonprofit umbrella agency. On the other side of the coin are the non-profits that are ineligible for government small-business loans yet cannot afford to borrow at current interest rates.

It is a sad commentary on our society, but the primary

reason for the lack of appropriate debate on quality child-care delivery is the myth that such services are only needed by the poor. "Many Americans have been under the misapprehension that . . . available services were used . . . largely by welfare families."[1] In fact, the opposite is true. Statistics from the National Center of Education reveal that less than 29 percent of families with incomes below $25,000 enrolled their 3- and 4-year-olds in preschool compared to 53 percent of families with incomes above $25,000.[2]

The fact of the matter is that the majority of parents have joined the child-care debate. And rightly so!

Day Care in the United States

The overwhelming majority of young children are being cared for formally and informally in family day-care homes. The estimates range from 3 to 5 million children. A mere 10 percent of these homes (140,000) are either licensed, certified, or otherwise registered. Fewer than 60,000 participate in the federal child-care food program.[3] The result—most of our children are spending the greater part of their days in an invisible underground without parental or regulatory oversight and access.

And of the more than two million U.S. employer companies, only about 500 to 600 offer some form of child-care support and up to half of these are hospitals.[4] Despite a variety of options—vouchers, information and referral, on-site centers—most employers are constrained by shortsighted state tax, fiscal, and other regulations. In Philadelphia, for example, one employer center costing $1.7 million with a licensed capacity of about 196 had to forego nonprofit status and subsequent incentives in order to serve its employees long-term and was forced to finance privately minus the advantage of low-interest rate loans because it did not qualify under the state regs as an "industrial" employer.[5]

There are approximately another 180,000 to 200,000 children being cared for in franchises or company-owned day care centers. Although licensed, these are plagued by high-staff turnover because of extremely low wages. In total, there are about 50,000 licensed day-care centers serving about two million children.[6] The major shift from care in one's own home to out-of-home care had occurred by the late seventies and is likely to continue. But despite a parallel increase in child-care services, the current supply is quite inadequate.

Day Care as an Enterprise

Despite a decrease in indirect public funding for child-care services, the 1981 Economic Recovery Tax Act did increase substantially the benefit for at least middle- and upper-income families. However, it is the moderate- and low-income families who are most burdened by child care costs. "There is growing pressure to make this tax credit refundable so that low-income families who do not owe taxes could receive it as a cash benefit,"[7] for example.

At a minimum, more attention should be paid to increasing the incentives for working parents to become providers of day care services. Already, in fact, day-care operators probably constitute the largest source of female entrepreneurs in this country. Well over 90 percent of those who are registered to provide day care are women.

Day-care enterprises can and should be part of neighborhood support systems. Not only would a formal strategy for infusing day care into neighborhood development increase local employment opportunities, it would enable low- and middle-income parents, especially single parents and women, to participate more fully in the economy. Local residents would become, in effect, both consumers and suppliers of this much needed service.

"For many low-income people, child care work is a way off welfare and into a career."[8] Organizations such as Montgomery's Federation of Child Care Centers of Alabama, Inc., was founded in 1971 to assist minority- and rural-owned and operated centers with exactly this type of career leap as well as with compliance with "stringent" state regulations.[9] By 1980, they had provided technical assistance to more than 79 local centers serving more than 5,000 children.

The fact of the matter is that most state regulations affecting child-care services—despite their intent—present major barriers to potential providers, whether they enter the marketplace as family home or center operators.

TABLE 2
Distribution of Children Aged Six and Under
of Working Women*

Type of child care by employ- ment status of mother	% 1977**	% 1965
Full-Time		
Care in child's home	28.6	47.2
By father	10.6	10.3
By other relative	11.4	18.4
By nonrelative	6.6	18.5
Care in another home	47.4	37.3
By relative	20.8	17.6
By nonrelative	26.6	19.6
Group care center	14.6	8.2
Child cares for self	0.3	0.3
Mother cares for child		
while working	8.2	6.7
All other arrangements	0.8	0.4
Total	100	100
Part-Time		
Care in child's home	42.7	47.0
By father	23.1	22.9
By other relative	11.2	15.6
By nonrelative	8.4	8.6
Care in another home	28.8	17.0
By relative	13.2	9.1
By nonrelative	15.6	7.9
Group care center	9.1	2.7
Child cares for self	0.5	0.9
Mother cares for child		
while working	18.5	32.3
All other arrangements	0.4	0.0
Total	100	100

*Married and once-married women.

**Data are only for the two youngest children under five years old.

Source: U.S. Bureau of the Census, *Trends in Child Care Arrangements of Working Mothers*, (Washington, D.C.: U.S. Government Printing Office, 1983), p. 6.

Removal of Barriers

Many initiatives by parents and groups to solve their own problems are hampered and frustrated by licensing requirements, regulations, and codes. Regulations and the process for enforcing them reduce the effectiveness and sometimes destroy the very existence of grassroots institutions and small businesses.

Very often these regulations do not provide effective or even reasonable levels of protection and benefits to vulnerable groups such as children. Nonetheless, many *do* provide substantial protections and benefits to professionals and bureaucrats. When regulations, licensing requirements, and codes are impediments to the initiatives of individuals and groups in developing and implementing self-help child care programs and strategies, then these barriers to self-help should be removed. Such a removal would be parallel to current efforts at deregulation in the economic arena. This strategy in no way suggests the removal of *all* social regulation. There are instances where regulations should be reformed rather than removed.

Among those regulations that should be scrutinized are professional licensing, restrictive zoning and building codes, as well as excessive administrative requirements. The removal of these barriers would release the vitality and ingenuity of existing institutions and also open up new institutions.

For example, in many cities, churches, and individuals willing to use their homes for delivering day care services are numerous. Indeed, we know that the vast majority of the U.S. families in the past have successfully handled the necessary care for their small children in informal settings in their immediate neighborhoods. There is also ample evidence that, if given the choice, most Americans today would prefer to continue using such informal arrangements, because they allow them direct knowledge of and control over the care of their children. These neighborhood individuals and groups represent an asset to local governments beset with financial problems and limited funding for government-provided day care services.

Yet, zoning regulations, staff requirements, and building codes that are designed for public elementary schools are applied to day-care facilities. Compliance has hampered many neighborhoods in their effort to start new day-care programs in residentially zoned areas. Only after protracted and expensive legal battles with zoning authorities can these day-care facilities operate.

Churches are also plagued by the compliance costs of certain regulations. Some have escalated monthly tuition costs per child by requiring such things as 60-square-feet per child for exterior (playground) space, one child-size toilet per ten children and reserved parking spaces for staff, or for staff with master's degrees in early childhood education. These requirements often add as much as $50 to $100 per child per month tuition costs, making it difficult to keep total costs below $200 per child per month.[10]

Case studies of individuals frustrated and confused by regulations abound. One day-care operator was given 48 hours to make structural changes in her house in order to keep her facility operating and to avoid criminal penalties. After borrowing $2,000 and making the changes, no one ever came to inspect. Another operator used her life savings to comply with requirements specified by an inspector, only to have her facility rejected by the city for noncompliance.[11]

Public policy must address the issue of whether the legal protections and quality controls are effective, logical, and have reasonable costs. Some of these regulations defy logic, but persist in spite of the horror stories. The sanity lapse of many day care regulations in Washington, D.C., was highlighted by one irate day-care operator who testified before a zoning board:

You're telling us that we cannot operate a day care facility in a residentially zoned middle-class neighborhood with a large number of working mothers, but we can operate a center in a commercial zone between two topless bars.[12]

Small business development barriers deserve special scrutiny also. The important role of small business in job creation is underscored by the following: Small businesses, which are generally classified as firms employing less than 500 people, comprise 98.2 percent of the nation's nonfarm businesses. These 10.8 million small businesses are this country's largest industrial and employment infrastructure, and direct or indirect livelihood for more than 100 million U. S. citizens. Yet, despite the importance of small-business development and survival in job creation, complying with a myriad of government regulations costs small business much more per dollar of revenue than it costs moderate or large-sized firms.

Of course, the removal of barriers alone will not suffice. Incentive is needed.

Promoting Innovation

The intent of most regulation of day care is to assure the "best" conditions for the health and safety of children. Increasingly, governments are recognizing that parents themselves are the best advocates for their children. And, "insofar as professional services and agencies have to be involved in the process of child care, they should be ancillary to the family and as far as possible be held accountable to parents."[13] How are we to accomplish this lofty goal and simultaneously encourage private and public sector support—at all levels of government—for expanding access to and increasing the options for quality child care services?

At a minimum, the child-care debate must address such questions as:

- Which day care models are most appropriate to implement at the neighborhood level? How do these reflect and impact the local values, character, and economies?
- What are the barriers to the provision of child-care services by locally based entrepreneurs?
- Which day-care delivery models strengthen the family?
- What are the features of appropriate professional supports that enhance parental rights?
- What constitutes useful training for providers, child development professionals, and parents?

The Economic Recovery Act of 1981 contains tax incentives, for example, for corporations to provide day-care centers at the work site; to purchase slots in established day-care centers; to provide cash or vouchers for day-care to employees; to provide in-kind services to community day care programs; and to provide day care information and referral services.

- Are corporations taking advantage of these incentives? If not, why not? What incentives would encourage corporate-sponsored day care? Are workers reluctant to

use corporate-sponsored day care? If so, why?
• Is the provision of day-care centers the best model for corporate support? Would other provisions—flextime, job sharing, part-time employment, paid maternity or paternity leave, cafeteria plans—be more in keeping with the mediating structures model?

Child-care tax credits are a move in the right direction. But instead of looking at them as revenue protection as most legislators do, there needs to be a more macroeconomic analysis of tax credits. For sure, most poor consumers of child care services will never qualify for the maximum tax credit benefit.

The six jurisdictions comprising the Greater Washington, D. C. Metropolitan Area—the District of Columbia, Alexandria and Arlington, Fairfax, Va.; Montgomery and Prince George's counties in Maryland—spent $16 million to subsidize day care for 7,600 children in 1981. They estimated an expenditure in 1983 of $18 million for 7,900 children.[14]

If these areas are typical, local governments are subsidizing day-care services at an annual rate of $2,100 to $2,500 per child served. And with the one exception of Fairfax County, most of this subsidy is for center care. Forty-five percent of the subsidy in Fairfax is for children served in family day-care homes.[15] Thus, it is obvious that the invisible underground serving most of our children—at least in Metropolitan Washington, D.C.—is economically self-sustaining. Clearly parents and providers are subsidizing the care of children—and at great personal sacrifice.

It is imperative, therefore, that strategies and policies be implemented that formally bring the family day-care homes into the marketplace. Barriers and disincentives must be removed in an effort to increase both the supply of quality service as well as the opportunity for the creation of competitive neighborhood-based businesses. Privatization is no panacea but simply because a particular social need is identified as a governmental responsibility, it does *not* follow that every program designed to meet this need must be either governmentally developed and/or implemented. On the contrary, research documents the fact that solutions designed by those experiencing the problems are not only the most cost effective and innovative but best all around.

Central to this approach is a belief in the capacity of people, however poor or underprivileged, to take control of their lives.

The political opportunity of the present moment lies in a public opinion that is eagerly ready for local common sense day care. A local official could build a powerful campaign on removing restrictive local regulations.

Notes

[1]Sheila B. Kamerman, "Working Mothers vs. America," *Working Woman,* November 1983, p. 131.

[2]*Ibid.* p. 132.

[3]Diane Adams, "Community Coordinated Child Care," in *National Day Care Home Study, 1982,* Madison, Wisconsin. U.S. Department of Health and Human Services.

[4]Diane Adams, "Administration for Children, Youth and Families, National Employer-Supported Child Care Project," *National Day Care Home Study,* 1982, U.S. Department of Health and Human Services.

[5]Conversation with Peter Aborn, Institute for Scientific Information, Philadelphia, April 1984.

[6]Diane Adams, *op. cit.*

[7]Sheila Kamerman, *op. cit.,* p. 134.

[8]Robert L. Woodson, *The Child Care Handbook: Needs Programs and Possibilities,* Children's Defense Fund, (Washington, D.C.: 1982, p. 68.)

[9]*Ibid.*

[10]American Enterprise Institute, Unpublished Survey of Day Care services in Washington, D.C.; 1980.

[11]*Ibid.*

[12]*Ibid.*

[13]Brigitte Berger and Sidney Callahan, eds., *Child Care and Mediating Structures* (Washington, D.C.: American Enterprise Institute, 1979), p. 13.

[14]Joan Maxwell, *Day Care: The Role of Washington-Area Local Governments* (Washington, D.C.: Greater Washington Research Center, 1982), p. ix.

[15]*Ibid.,* p. 11.